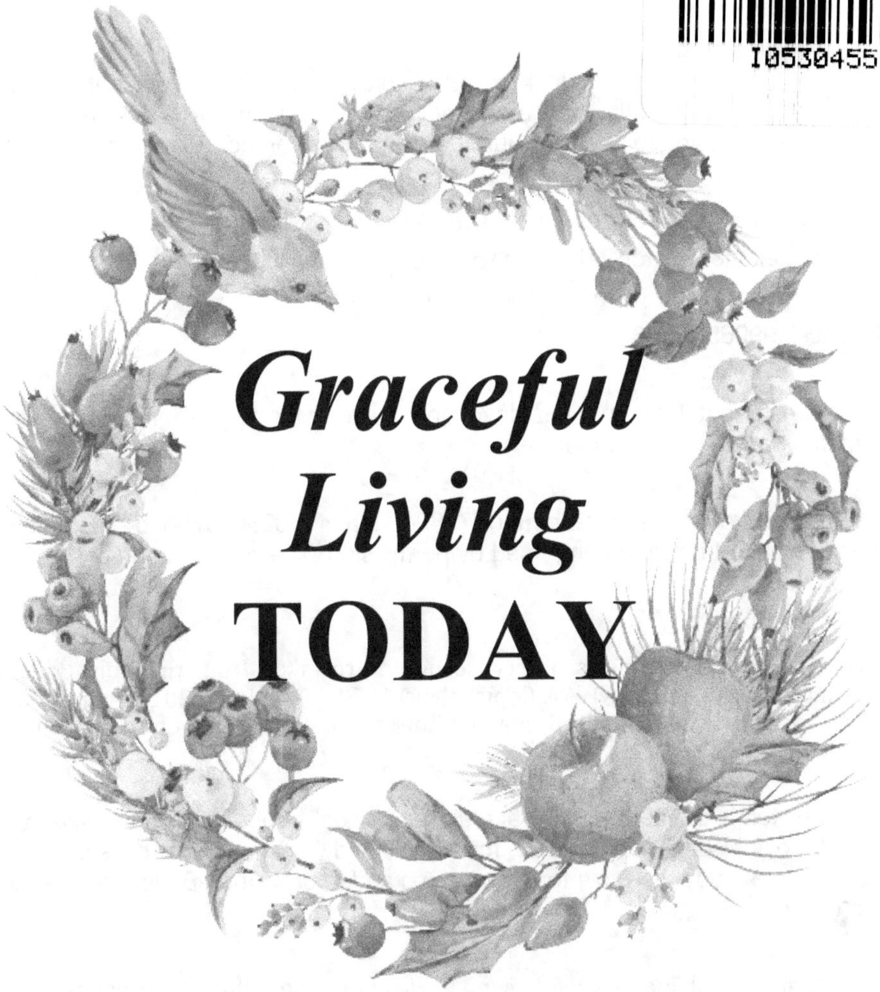

Graceful Living TODAY

150 Bible-rich, Christ-focused
devotions for a joy-filled life

MELANIE NEWTON

JOYFUL
WALK
BIBLE
STUDIES

We extend our heartfelt thanks to Tim Stevenson who created the original T.E.A.M. Training course on which the core of this devotional is based. We also extend an extra special thank you to Michelle Burns for serving as an editor for this devotional.

Graceful Living Today: 150 Bible-rich, Christ-focused devotions for a joy-filled life
© 2025 by Melanie Newton. All rights reserved.
Published by Joyful Walk Press. Flower Mound, TX.
ISBN: 979-8-9926517-0-6

For questions about the use of this devotional guide or for bulk orders, please email us at melanienewton.com/contact.

Cover adapted from a watercolor image (569e9d1a5404398c067b61b452c825a8.png) accessed online at i.pinimg.com, used by permission. The original source of this image was not found.

Melanie Newton is the author of "Graceful Beginnings" books for anyone new to the Bible and "Joyful Walk Bible Studies" for established Christians. Her mission is to help women learn to study the Bible for themselves and to grow their Bible-teaching skills to lead others.

We pray that you will find *Graceful Living Today* a resource that God will use to strengthen you in your faith walk with God.

Christ-Focused • Grace-Based • Bible-Rich

JOYFUL WALK PRESS
Flower Mound, TX

MELANIE NEWTON

Melanie Newton is a Louisiana girl who made the choice to follow Jesus while attending LSU. She and her husband Ron married and moved to Texas for him to attend Dallas Theological Seminary. They stayed in Texas where Ron led a wilderness camping ministry for troubled youth for many years. Ron now helps corporations with their challenging employees and is the author of the top-rated business book, *No Jerks on the Job*.

Melanie jumped into raising three Texas-born children and serving in ministry to women at her church. Through the years, the Lord has given her opportunity to do Bible teaching and to write grace-based Bible studies for women that are now available from her website (melanienewton.com) and on Bible.org. *Graceful Beginnings* books are for anyone new to the Bible. *Joyful Walk Bible Studies* are for maturing Christians.

Melanie Newton loves to help women learn how to study the Bible for themselves. She also teaches online courses for women to grow their Bible-teaching skills to help others—all with the goal of getting to know Jesus more along the way. Her heart's desire is to encourage you to have a joyful relationship with Jesus Christ so you are willing to share that experience with others around you.

Jesus took hold of me in 1972, and I've been on this great adventure ever since. My life is a gift of God, full of blessings in the midst of difficult challenges. The more I've learned and experienced God's absolutely amazing grace, the more I've discovered my faith walk to be a joyful one. I'm still seeking that joyful walk every day...

Melanie

OTHER BIBLE STUDIES BY MELANIE NEWTON

Graceful Beginnings books for anyone new to the Bible:
A Fresh Start (basics for new Christians)
Painting the Portrait of Jesus (the Gospel of John)
The God You Can Know (the character of God)
Grace Overflowing (an overview of Paul's 13 letters)
The Walk from Fear to Faith (7 Old Testament women)
Satisfied by His Love (women who knew Jesus)
Seek the Treasure (study of Ephesians)
Pathways to a Joyful Walk (6 pathways to a joy-filled life)

Joyful Walk Bible Studies for growing Christians:
Adorn Yourself with Godliness (1 Timothy and Titus, also in Spanish)
Everyday Women, Ever Faithful God (Old Testament women, also in Spanish)
Connecting Faith to Life on Planet Earth (Genesis 1-11; Revelation)
Graceful Living (the essentials for a grace-based Christian life)
Graceful Living Today (a Bible-rich, Christ-focused devotional for a joyful life)
Healthy Living (Colossians and Philemon)
Heartbreak to Hope (the Gospel of Mark)
Identity: Sticking to Your Faith in a Pull-Apart World (Ezra thru Malachi)
Knowing Jesus, Knowing Joy (Philippians, also in Spanish)
Live Out His Love (New Testament women)
Perspective (1and 2 Thessalonians)
Profiles of Perseverance (Old Testament men, also in Spanish)
Radical Acts (Acts)
Reboot, Renew, Rejoice (1 and 2 Chronicles)
The God-Dependent Woman (2 Corinthians)
To Be Found Faithful (2 Timothy)

Resources for leading others
Be a Christ-Focused Small Group Leader
Leap into Lifestyle Disciplemaking
Painting the Picture of Jesus (the "I Am's" of Jesus lessons for children)
Teaching Children the God They Can Know (the character of God for children)

Download our catalogue and get resources for your spiritual growth at melanienewton.com.

Contents

INTRODUCTION TO GRACEFUL LIVING

Jesus Christ presented Himself as the answer to every need of the human heart. The New Testament writers unanimously taught the same. Multitudes of people throughout the centuries since have witnessed that He does indeed do what He promised for those who trust and follow Him.

I have been a Jesus follower for more than 40 years now. Not once have I regretted that decision. I am a lifelong learner, a student of God's Word and my Lord's life. He teaches me in many ways.

Recently, someone asked me, "How has Jesus discipled you? What has made the most impact on my life?" When it comes to knowing who I am and where I stand with my God, without a doubt, the best teaching I have had was that which effectively covered the foundational principles of Christianity—who Christ is, what He accomplished on the cross for us, what the resurrection means for us, and our identity in Him.

That wonderful teaching communicated clearly and succinctly to me what I needed to know to live dependently on Christ and rest in my assurance of life **in** Him and through Him. I learned more about the purpose for the cross and the resurrection than I had ever heard before. I learned how to recognize the poison of legalism in a Christian's life. It was through this teaching that I became aware that my flesh is not getting better the longer I know Christ. I need to depend 100% on Him now as I ever did as a young believer in the 1970s.

These timeless truths are essential for every believer to enjoy the life God has planned for them. So I've adapted the original teaching I received (given as a series of lectures) into a Bible study called *Graceful Living*. This devotional *Graceful Living Today* teaches the same content but in small daily portions.

It is critically important for those who know Christ to have sound theology (rational, systematic understanding of God). Theology is inescapable. Any thoughts you have about God or information you receive about God is theology.

We live according to our theology. Our theology can be based on truth or error. Truth and error lead to dramatically different results. Jesus promised to anyone who believes in Him that if you hold to His teaching, you will know the truth, which will set you free (John 8:31-32). If truth sets you free, then the opposite is also true. It is error that binds you.

Jesus Christ invites you to follow Him in discipleship—not to imprison you, but to give you abundant life and rest for your soul. What Jesus offers to His followers is life **full of His grace**. What is God's grace? Grace is commonly defined as unmerited favor…an undeserved gift. It is God's gift to an undeserving mankind. God gives His grace because of His great love and mercy. Understanding God's grace given to you is essential to enjoying the life that God has planned for you.

The heart of *Graceful Living Today* is the message of God's love and grace in Jesus Christ and the reality of Christ alive and living in you. This Bible-rich, Christ-focused devotional will help you build a foundation for joyful Christian living based on God's grace to you and for you. As you apply these truths in your life, you will experience graceful living—a joy-filled life overflowing with His grace.

May our grace-giving God fill your heart and mind with His grace so that you will enjoy the life that He has planned for you.

HOW TO USE THIS DEVOTIONAL BOOK

Have you ever wondered why books such as this one are called "devotionals?" The word devotional comes from "devotion." The word devotion means profound dedication, commitment, and earnest attachment to a cause or person. For a devotional such as *Graceful Living Today*, its purpose is to increase your devotion, commitment, and attachment to God. Devotion to God means you are dedicated to Him. You are firmly attached to Him. Whatever He wants, you want. It is a loyal love for God.

A devotional is not a daily "to do" that you can check off your list because Christians are supposed to do them. A devotional is not supposed to make you feel better about yourself or learn a way to fix a problem in your life. A devotional is an intentional act on your part to express and build upon your devotion to God, your love for Him, and your loyalty to Him. Out of this devotion to God should come a desire to live the life He has planned for you. That will always be a life that is pleasing to Him. We hope that *Graceful Living Today* will not only grow your devotion to God but also result in a life that reflects your love for Him in every way.

Some Bible Basics

Throughout these lessons, you will use a Bible to answer questions as you discover treasure about your life with Christ. The Bible is one book containing a collection of 66 books combined together for our benefit. It is divided into two main parts: The Old Testament and the New Testament.

The Old Testament tells the story of the beginning of the world and God's promises to mankind given through the nation of Israel. It tells how the people of Israel obeyed and disobeyed God over many, many years. All the stories and messages in the Old Testament lead up to Jesus Christ's coming to the earth.

The New Testament tells the story of Jesus Christ, the early Christians, and God's promises to all those who believe in Jesus. You can think of the Old Testament as "before Christ" and the New Testament as "after Christ."

Each book of the Bible is divided into chapters and verses within those chapters to make it easier to study. Bible references include the book name, chapter number and verse number(s). For example, Ephesians 2:8 refers to the New Testament book of Ephesians, the 2nd chapter, and verse 8 within that 2nd chapter. Printed Bibles have a "Table of Contents" in the front to help you locate books by page number. Bible apps also have a contents list by book and chapter.

The Bible verses highlighted in each lesson in this study are from the New International Version® (NIV®) unless otherwise indicated. Also, this study capitalizes certain pronouns referring to God, Jesus and the Holy Spirit—He, Him, His, Himself—just to make the reading of the textual information less confusing. Some Bible translations likewise capitalize those pronouns referring to God; others do not. It is simply a matter of preference, not a requirement. We do it to make it easy for you to follow.

What to Expect Each Day

This book is divided into 150 days covering 11 main aspects of God's amazing grace toward you as you live your Christian life. These are what God in His great love has done for you. They are part of God's plan for you to experience His love, His freedom, and His joy every day as you live in His grace.

Each daily topic builds upon the one before it. Unlike typical devotionals which are mostly commentary, this devotional book invites you to participate in reading the truth of God's Word and responding to it. That is why it is not only a daily devotional but is also a guided study for you to grow in your faith.

Give yourself 10-15 minutes to work through each daily devotional, which includes 4 sections:

1. Read the Truth

You read specifically chosen Bible verses related to the focus of the day. You can read the verses in any translation you choose. We have included the verses (NIV) in this book so you can readily see them without having to go between two sources such as an app or website and this book.

2. Confirm the Truth

After you've read the Scriptures, you can answer simple questions based on what the biblical text actually says. It is very important to see what the Bible actually says and not just go by what you may have heard about it. This "Observation" step is the most important step in the process of Bible Study. Reading the verse and answering the question based upon that verse will confirm that truth in your mind.

3. Understand the Truth

The wording in this section continues to confirm what you just read for yourself and expands the teaching to help you understand what it means. That's the "Interpretation" step in the process of Bible Study. Further explanation, if needed, is given in this section so that you can truly understand the truth of what the Bible says. The focus is always what the Scripture says more than anyone's commentary on it.

4. Reflect and Respond

This is the devotion part. There is space for you to add your own personal reflection on the day's teaching. You get to reflect on what you just learned about your life as a believer in Christ and respond to God through whatever means you choose—writing, speaking to God (prayer), or any creative means. You also get to decide how you should apply what you learned in your own life. This is the "Application" step in the process of Bible Study. On some days, I offer up some prompting questions for you to consider. God reveals truth in His Word. You are to respond to Him and what He has revealed to you. This increases your devotion to Him.

Doing This as a Group?

If you are working through this devotional with someone else or with a group, we recommend that you get together once a week and discuss what everyone learned in the 7 daily devotionals for the week.

Enjoy!

May your love for God grow by leaps and bounds as you learn how to live in His amazing grace today, tomorrow, and every day of the rest of your earthly life.

part 1

GOD'S INVITATION TO A LIFE OF FREEDOM AND JOY

To the Jews who had believed Him, Jesus said, "If you hold to my teaching, you are really my disciples. Then you will know the truth, and the truth will set you free." (John 8:31-32)

"Come to me, all you who are weary and burdened, and I will give you rest. Take my yoke upon you and learn from me, for I am gentle and humble in heart, and you will find rest for your souls. For my yoke is easy and my burden is light." (Matthew 11:28-30)

DAY 1

GOD'S INVITATION TO THE LIFE HE HAS PLANNED FOR YOU

Read the Truth

"The thief comes only to steal and kill and destroy; I have come that they [His followers] may have life, and have it to the full." (John 10:10)

"Come to me, all you who are weary and burdened, and I will give you rest. Take my yoke upon you and learn from me, for I am gentle and humble in heart, and you will find rest for your souls. For my yoke is easy and my burden is light." (Matthew 11:28-30)

Confirm the Truth

What does Jesus promise to you in John 10:10?

What does Jesus promise to you in Matthew 11:28-30?

Understand the Truth

Jesus Christ presented Himself as the answer to every need of the human heart. The New Testament writers confirmed that truth in their teaching. Multitudes of people throughout the centuries since have witnessed that Jesus does indeed do what He promised for those who trust and follow Him. He will do this for you.

Jesus offers us "full" life (John 10:10). Full is not empty. Full means to have purpose and meaning. Full does not mean easy, though. Fullness means that even when we are weary and burdened (Matthew 11:28-30), we can go to Him with open hands and receive the rest and guidance that He readily gives. Jesus' invitation says, "Come to me. Connect to me. Learn from me. Rest with me." That sounds pretty wonderful.

Jesus Christ invites you to a life of fullness, freedom and joy. This is the kind of life God has planned for you. Are you interested?

Reflect and Respond

6

GOD'S INVITATION TO THE LIFE HE HAS PLANNED FOR YOU

Read the Truth

To the Jews who had believed Him, Jesus said, "If you hold to my teaching, you are really my disciples. Then you will know the truth, and the truth will set you free." (John 8:31-32)

Confirm the Truth

What does Jesus promise to you in John 8:31-32?

Understand the Truth

It is critically important for anyone who knows Christ to have sound theology (rational, systematic understanding of God). Theology is inescapable. Any thoughts you have about God or information you receive about God is theology. We live according to our theology.

Our theology can be based on truth or error. Truth and error lead to dramatically different results. If truth sets you free, then the opposite is also true. It is error that binds you. When you know the truth that is revealed to you in the Bible, you will experience freedom. With freedom comes a life of joy. this is the kind of life God has planned for you. Do you want a life of joy? Stand firmly on God's truth revealed to you in His Word, the Bible.

Reflect and Respond

GOD'S INVITATION TO THE LIFE HE HAS PLANNED FOR YOU

Read the Truth

From the fullness of His grace we have all received one blessing after another. For the law was given through Moses; grace and truth came through Jesus Christ. (John 1:16-17)

Confirm the Truth

What have you received from God?

Understand the Truth

Jesus Christ invites you to follow Him in discipleship—not to imprison you but to give you abundant life and rest for your soul. What Jesus offers to His followers is life **full of grace**. What is grace? In particular, what is God's grace?

Grace is commonly defined as unmerited favor…an undeserved gift. It is God's gift to an undeserving mankind. Understanding God's grace given to you is essential to enjoying the life that God has planned for you.

May our "Grace-giving" God completely fill your heart with His grace so that you become a "grace-sharer" in your life. "Graceful living" is life overflowing with His grace—**a life of freedom and joy!**

Reflect and Respond

part 2

CHRIST, THE GRACE-GIFT

From the fullness of His grace we have all received one blessing after another. For the law was given through Moses; grace and truth came through Jesus Christ. (John 1:16-17)

CHRISTIANITY IS CHRIST!

The New Testament opens with the births of John the Baptist and Jesus. About 30 years later, John challenged the Jews to indicate their repentance (turning from sin and toward God) by submitting to water baptism—a familiar Old Testament practice used for repentance. It was also used when a non-Jew (usually called Gentile) converted to Judaism. The water baptism represented being washed clean of idolatry.

Jesus is God's Son, fully God and fully man. Jesus publicly showed the world what God is like and taught God's perfect ways for more than 3 years. After preparing 12 disciples to continue His earthly work, He died voluntarily on a cross for human sin, rose from the dead, and returned to Heaven. The account of His earthly life is recorded in 4 books known as the Gospels, the biblical books of Matthew, Mark, Luke and John named after the compiler of each account.

Each Gospel presents Jesus as "the Christ." This title is from the Greek word *christos,* a translation of the Hebrew term "Messiah" meaning "anointed one." The Old Testament prophets promised that the Messiah, as the anointed one of God, would come and do many wonderful things for God's people, including restoring God's Kingdom on earth. Christians are followers of Jesus, who is the Christ.

Read the Truth

That power is the same as the mighty strength He exerted when He raised Christ from the dead and seated Him at His right hand in the heavenly realms, far above all rule and authority, power and dominion, and every name that is invoked, not only in the present age but also in the one to come. And God placed all things under His feet and appointed Him to be head over everything for the Church, which is His body, the fullness of Him who fills everything in every way. (Ephesians 1:19b-23)

Confirm the Truth

Where is Christ now?

What authority does He have?

What is His relationship to the Church?

Understand the Truth

If you have heard the good news of the Gospel and believed that Jesus is the Christ, the Son of God who gave Himself for your sins, you have eternal life just by believing in Him as the Savior. But more than salvation, Jesus Christ calls you into a relationship with Himself. Christianity is Christ! It is not a lifestyle, rules of conduct, or a society whose members were initiated by the sprinkling or covering of water. Christ calls us into a close relationship with Him as brothers, sisters, and friends.

Yet, He is also our Lord, the one who sits at the right hand of His Father God as head over everything else in heaven and on earth. As Lord, Jesus Christ is our *master*—the one to whom we should willingly give our obedience. He is our *model* of how to live as humans in a dependent relationship with God, and He is our *mentor* in walking with us in that dependent relationship.

Jesus' disciples 2000 years ago were no different than we are except they physically beheld the risen Christ. We must see Him through eyes of faith and allow the Gospels to leap off the page revealing our Lord so that we may know this God-man who changed our lives as we received the Good News. We need to frequently read the Gospels, watch movies based on them, and tell the stories about Jesus as often as needed to know His life well because …**Christianity is Christ!** Christ is the ultimate grace-gift to us.

Reflect and Respond

WHO IS JESUS?

Read the Truth

"Hear, O Israel! The LORD our God, the LORD is one! Love the LORD your God with all your heart and with all your soul and with all your strength." (Deuteronomy 6:4-5)

"You are my witnesses," declares the LORD, "and my servant whom I have chosen, so that you may know and believe me and understand that I am He. Before me no god was formed, nor will there be one after me. I, even I, am the LORD, and apart from me there is no savior." (Isaiah 43:10-11)

Confirm the Truth

What is declared about God in Deuteronomy 6:4-5?

What does God declare about Himself in Isaiah 43:10-11?

Understand the Truth

According to the Bible, God chose to reveal Himself to the nation of Israel and, through Israel, to the world. Many truths about God (His "attributes") are taught in the Bible. From both the Old Testament and the New Testament, we discover these truths about God. He is…

Creator	Unchangeable	Gracious	Good	Just	Love
Faithful	Omnipresent	All-knowing	Patient	Righteous	Holy
Forgiving	Compassionate	All-powerful	Merciful	Sovereign	Wise

But the one thing that is clearly and relentlessly asserted about God in the Old Testament is that there is only one true and living God. God commands that people worship Him only.

Jesus of Nazareth appeared and issued His challenge to the people living in a very religious culture. When He came on the scene, Jesus called people to a spiritual relationship with Himself and God the Father (John 17:3; Matthew 11:28-30). He claimed to be the answer to the needs of the human heart. Of all the world's religions, Jesus is the only "founder" who claimed to be equal with God. For the next few days, we will see what the Scripture says about who Jesus Christ is.

Reflect and Respond

WHAT JESUS CLAIMED ABOUT HIMSELF

Read the Truth

So because Jesus was doing these things on the Sabbath, the Jewish leaders began to persecute Him. In His defense Jesus said to them, "My Father is always at His work to this very day, and I too am working." For this reason, they tried all the more to kill Him; not only was He breaking the Sabbath, but He was even calling God His own Father, making Himself equal with God. (John 5:16-18)

Jesus gave them this answer: "Very truly I tell you, the Son can do nothing by Himself; He can do only what He sees His Father doing, because whatever the Father does the Son also does. For the Father loves the Son and shows Him all He does. Yes, and He will show Him even greater works than these, so that you will be amazed. For just as the Father raises the dead and gives them life, even so the Son gives life to whom He is pleased to give it. Moreover, the Father judges no one, but has entrusted all judgment to the Son, that all may honor the Son just as they honor the Father. Whoever does not honor the Son does not honor the Father, who sent Him. (John 5:19-23)

"Very truly I tell you, whoever hears my word and believes Him who sent me has eternal life and will not be judged but has crossed over from death to life. Very truly I tell you, a time is coming and has now come when the dead will hear the voice of the Son of God and those who hear will live. For as the Father has life in Himself, so He has granted the Son also to have life in Himself. And He has given Him authority to judge because He is the Son of Man. (John 5:24-27)

Confirm the Truth

What does Jesus claim about Himself in John 5:16-18?

What does Jesus claim about Himself in John 5:19-23?

What does Jesus claim about Himself in John 5:24-27?

Understand the Truth

John chapter 5 is a long dialogue between Jesus and the Jewish leaders. In it, Jesus states many truths about Himself that are clues to His being not only the promised Messiah, but also God in the flesh (human body). Did you notice that Jesus called God His Father, claiming He was equal with God as

13

God's Son? He also claims to give life to whomever He is pleased to give it. Only God gives life. All judgment has been entrusted to Him. Only God is the judge of human destiny. And Jesus says that He deserves the honor that belongs to God, including worship, which He accepted without restraint.

Reflect and Respond

WHAT JESUS CLAIMED ABOUT HIMSELF

Read the Truth

"I have testimony weightier than that of John [the Baptist]. For the works that the Father has given me to finish—the very works that I am doing—testify that the Father has sent me. And the Father who sent me has Himself testified concerning me. You have never heard His voice nor seen His form, nor does His word dwell in you, for you do not believe the one He sent. You study the Scriptures diligently because you think that in them you have eternal life. These are the very Scriptures that testify about me, yet you refuse to come to me to have life." (John 5:36-40)

"But do not think I will accuse you before the Father. Your accuser is Moses, on whom your hopes are set. If you believed Moses, you would believe me, for he wrote about me." (John 5:45-46)

Confirm the Truth

What does Jesus claim about Himself in John 5:36-40?

What does Jesus claim about Himself in John 5:45-46?

Understand the Truth

In this part of John chapter 5, Jesus continues His dialogue with the Jewish leaders and everyone else who was listening to this "sermon." He has called God His Father, equates Himself with someone who can give life, declares His right to judge, and accepts worship and honor. Now, He appeals to the audience to view the work He's been doing as evidence that He has been sent by the Father. The Scriptures testify about Him, and Moses Himself wrote about Him. Like a lawyer trying a case, Jesus presents undeniable evidence that He is Messiah and the Son of God.

Reflect and Respond

WHAT JESUS CLAIMED ABOUT HIMSELF

Read the Truth

A few days later, when Jesus again entered Capernaum, the people heard that he had come home. They gathered in such large numbers that there was no room left, not even outside the door, and He preached the word to them. Some men came, bringing to him a paralyzed man, carried by four of them. Since they could not get him to Jesus because of the crowd, they made an opening in the roof above Jesus by digging through it and then lowered the mat the man was lying on. When Jesus saw their faith, He said to the paralyzed man, "Son, your sins are forgiven." Now some teachers of the law were sitting there, thinking to themselves, "Why does this fellow talk like that? He's blaspheming! Who can forgive sins but God alone?" Immediately Jesus knew in His spirit that this was what they were thinking in their hearts, and He said to them, "Why are you thinking these things? Which is easier: to say to this paralyzed man, 'Your sins are forgiven,' or to say, 'Get up, take your mat and walk'? But I want you to know that the Son of Man has authority on earth to forgive sins." So He said to the man, "I tell you, get up, take your mat and go home." He got up, took his mat and walked out in full view of them all. This amazed everyone and they praised God, saying, "We have never seen anything like this!" (Mark 2:1-12)

Confirm the Truth

What right or authority does Jesus claim in Mark 2:1-12?

Understand the Truth

In Mark 2, Jesus forgave the paralyzed man's sins. By doing so, He made claim to the divine right and authority to forgive sins. Only God can forgive sins. The teachers of the Law knew that only God could forgive sins. They recognized Jesus' claim to the authority of God. He declared to them and to us, "I want you to know that the Son of Man has authority on earth to forgive sins." Jesus was not just a good teacher. He claimed and demonstrated that He was God in human flesh.

Reflect and Respond

WHAT JESUS CLAIMED ABOUT HIMSELF

Read the Truth

They sailed to the region of the Gerasenes, which is across the lake from Galilee. When Jesus stepped ashore, He was met by a demon-possessed man from the town. For a long time this man had not worn clothes or lived in a house, but had lived in the tombs. When he saw Jesus, he cried out and fell at His feet, shouting at the top of his voice, "What do you want with me, Jesus, Son of the Most High God? I beg you, don't torture me!" For Jesus had commanded the impure spirit to come out of the man. Many times it had seized him, and though he was chained hand and foot and kept under guard, he had broken his chains and had been driven by the demon into solitary places. Jesus asked him, "What is your name?" "Legion," he replied, because many demons had gone into him. And they begged Jesus repeatedly not to order them to go into the Abyss. A large herd of pigs was feeding there on the hillside. The demons begged Jesus to let them go into the pigs, and He gave them permission. When the demons came out of the man, they went into the pigs, and the herd rushed down the steep bank into the lake and was drowned. (Luke 8:26-33)

Confirm the Truth

What right or authority does Jesus demonstrate in Luke 8:26-33?

Understand the Truth

In Luke 8, Jesus demonstrates authority over demons and can determine their destiny. He commanded the impure spirits to come out of the man. He has the ability to choose where they will go. Jesus could send them to the Abyss, a place where God has imprisoned many demons. Only God can send demons to the Abyss. But after they asked Him not to do that, Jesus chose to send them into the pigs. Notice that they were not given permission by Jesus to go back into the man.

Reflect and Respond

WHAT JESUS CLAIMED ABOUT HIMSELF

Read the Truth

Now on His way to Jerusalem, Jesus traveled along the border between Samaria and Galilee. As He was going into a village, ten men who had leprosy met Him. They stood at a distance and called out in a loud voice, "Jesus, Master, have pity on us!" When He saw them, He said, "Go, show yourselves to the priests." And as they went, they were cleansed. One of them, when he saw he was healed, came back, praising God in a loud voice. He threw himself at Jesus' feet and thanked Him—and he was a Samaritan. Jesus asked, "Were not all ten cleansed? Where are the other nine? Has no one returned to give praise to God except this foreigner?" Then He said to him, "Rise and go; your faith has made you well." (Luke 17:11-19)

Very truly I tell you, whoever believes in me will do the works I have been doing, and they will do even greater things than these, because I am going to the Father. And I will do whatever you ask in my name, so that the Father may be glorified in the Son. You may ask me for anything in my name, and I will do it. (John 14:12-14)

Confirm the Truth

What right or authority does Jesus demonstrate in Luke 17:11-19?

What right or authority does Jesus demonstrate in John 14:12-14?

Understand the Truth

In Luke 17, Jesus not only displayed authority over leprosy, an incurable disease, but He also accepted worship from one of those who was healed. The healed man, who was not Jewish, threw himself at Jesus' feet and thanked Him. Jesus did not tell him to stop but accepted the worship. He then asked why the rest of the healed didn't recognize the work of God on their behalf and likewise offer their thanks. In John 14, Jesus claimed the authority to answer prayer. Only God can promise to answer anyone's prayer. And prayer can be asked in Jesus' name, stating He has that authority as well. Yet, His purpose in doing this is so that His Father can be glorified (praised) and made known for the work that He does. Prayer is very personal. Jesus is a personal Savior offering to meet personal needs of those who love Him. What a joy!

Reflect and Respond

18

DAY 11

WHAT JESUS CLAIMED ABOUT HIMSELF

Read the Truth

Then Jesus declared, "I am the bread of life. Whoever comes to me will never go hungry, and whoever believes in me will never be thirsty. (John 6:35)

All those the Father gives me will come to me, and whoever comes to me I will never drive away. For I have come down from heaven not to do my will but to do the will of Him who sent me. (John 6:37-38)

And this is the will of Him who sent me, that I shall lose none of all those He has given me, but raise them up at the last day. For my Father's will is that everyone who looks to the Son and believes in Him shall have eternal life, and I will raise them up at the last day." (John 6:39-40)

Confirm the Truth

What does Jesus promise in John 6:35?

From where does Jesus say He has come and why (John 6:37-38)?

What does Jesus claim in John 6:39-40?

Understand the Truth

Not only does Jesus promise to meet the spiritual hunger and thirst of everyone who comes to Him (John 6:35), but He also claims to have come down from heaven and to have been sent by God the Father (John 6:37-38). This is a claim of pre-existence, that is, Jesus is claiming to have existed before His human birth. Jesus goes on to say that He has been sent by His Father to do the Father's will on earth. That will is to draw people to God and have authority over their eternal destiny. Only God has authority over eternal destiny. Jesus Christ is God.

Reflect and Respond

19

WHAT JESUS CLAIMED ABOUT HIMSELF

Read the Truth

Jesus replied, "If I glorify myself, my glory means nothing. My Father, whom you claim as your God, is the one who glorifies me. Though you do not know Him, I know Him. If I said I did not, I would be a liar like you, but I do know Him and obey His word. Your father Abraham rejoiced at the thought of seeing my day; he saw it and was glad." "You are not yet fifty years old," they said to Him, "and you have seen Abraham!" "Very truly I tell you," Jesus answered, "before Abraham was born, I am!" At this, they picked up stones to stone Him, but Jesus hid Himself, slipping away from the temple grounds. (John 8:54-59)

"And now, Father, glorify me in your presence with the glory I had with you before the world began." (John 17:5)

"Father, I want those you have given me to be with me where I am, and to see my glory, the glory you have given me because you loved me before the creation of the world." (John 17:24)

Confirm the Truth

What does Jesus claim about His pre-existence in John 8:54-59?

What does Jesus claim about His pre-existence in John 17:5?

What does Jesus claim about His relationship with God in John 17:24?

Understand the Truth

In John 8, Jesus says that He knows God, adding that He had known Abraham 2000 years before this time. Jesus followed up with, "Before Abraham was born, I am." That "I am" was the name by which the Jews knew their God—in Hebrew, *Yahweh*. Jesus claimed to be God Himself. That infuriated the listeners. But there was no question about it. Jesus claimed it without hesitation regardless of the danger to Himself.

Twice in the beautiful prayer of John 17, Jesus spoke about the relationship He had with His Father before He was sent to earth and even before the world was created. Together, they had existed in a special relationship—a relationship of love between the Father and the Son. From this love relationship flows the love that Jesus has for all those who follow Him.

Reflect and Respond

WHAT JESUS CLAIMED ABOUT HIMSELF

Read the Truth

So Jesus said, "When you have lifted up the Son of Man, then you will know that I am He and that I do nothing on my own but speak just what the Father has taught me. The one who sent me is with me; He has not left me alone, for I always do what pleases Him." (John 8:28-29)

Jesus said to them, "If God were your Father, you would love me, for I have come here from God. I have not come on my own; God sent me. (John 8:42)

Why is my language not clear to you? Because you are unable to hear what I say. You belong to your father, the devil, and you want to carry out your father's desires. He was a murderer from the beginning, not holding to the truth, for there is no truth in him. When he lies, he speaks his native language, for he is a liar and the father of lies. Yet because I tell the truth, you do not believe me! Can any of you prove me guilty of sin? If I am telling the truth, why don't you believe me? Whoever belongs to God hears what God says. The reason you do not hear is that you do not belong to God." (John 8:43-47)

Confirm the Truth

What did Jesus claim about Himself in John 8:28-29?

What did Jesus claim about Himself in John 8:42?

What did Jesus claim about Himself in John 8:43-47?

Understand the Truth

As you have already seen, Jesus Christ claimed to possess a unique relationship with God the Father, a unique authority from the Father, and to be the center and goal of the Hebrew Scriptures (the Old Testament). He accepted worship, claimed the authority to forgive sins and pronounce judgment, demonstrated authority over demonic powers and claimed the ability to answer prayer. In John 8, Jesus claims to speak what Father God has taught Him. He also claims to always do what pleases God. And no man can prove Him guilty of any sin. These are fantastic claims to make by anyone who was not absolutely certain that they are true. Jesus knew who He was. He knew His purpose.

Though Jesus was executed by Rome as a state criminal (the meaning of crucifixion), His innocence was repeatedly confirmed by others. Pontius Pilate said he could find no fault and no basis for a charge against Him (Luke 23:4,13-15,22). King Herod Antipas declared he could find no basis for a charge (Luke 23:8-12,15). The criminal crucified next to Jesus said that He did nothing wrong (Luke 23:41). And a Roman centurion declared Him "a righteous man" (Luke 23:47).

Reflect and Respond

WHAT JESUS CLAIMED ABOUT HIMSELF

Read the Truth

The LORD says to my Lord. "Sit at my right hand until I make your enemies a footstool for your feet." (Psalm 110:1)

In my vision at night I looked, and there before me was one like a son of man, coming with the clouds of heaven. He approached the Ancient of Days and was led into His presence. He was given authority, glory and sovereign power; all nations and peoples of every language worshiped Him. His dominion is an everlasting dominion that will not pass away, and His kingdom is one that will never be destroyed. (Daniel 7:13-14)

But Jesus remained silent and gave no answer. Again the high priest asked Him, "Are you the Messiah, the Son of the Blessed One?" "I am," said Jesus. "And you will see the Son of Man sitting at the right hand of the Mighty One and coming on the clouds of heaven." The high priest tore his clothes. "Why do we need any more witnesses?" he asked. "You have heard the blasphemy. What do you think?" They all condemned Him as worthy of death. (Mark 14:61-64)

Confirm the Truth

According to Psalm 110:1, what position of authority would the promised Messiah (my Lord) hold?

According to the vision in Daniel 7:13-14, how would the promised Messiah (my Lord) come to earth?

According to Daniel 7:13-14, what position of authority would the promised Messiah (son of man) hold?

What did Jesus claim about Himself regarding His being the promised Messiah in Mark 14:61-64?

Understand the Truth

The promised Messiah would be sitting at God's right hand and would have authority and sovereign power. Designated by Daniel's prophecy as "the Son of Man," He would be seen coming with, or on, the clouds of heaven. Jesus claimed these truths for Himself in the gospels. He called Himself the Son of Man (seen often in Luke's gospel). During His trial, Jesus said that He would be seen sitting at the right hand of God (fulfilling Psalm 110:1) and coming on the clouds of heaven (Daniel 7:13-14). There is absolutely no doubt that Jesus claimed to be God and to have the authority of God.

The coming of Jesus Christ into human history was not an event that suddenly burst upon an unsuspecting world. It was the fulfillment of a long line of prophecies that started with the beginning of human history in Genesis 3:15. (We'll look at this later.) The arrival of Jesus in human form was planned before the creation of the world as well as the mission He was sent to accomplish—reconciling the world to God.

Reflect and Respond

What Jesus Claimed about Himself

Read the Truth

When Jesus came to the region of Caesarea Philippi, He asked His disciples, "Who do people say the Son of Man is?" They replied, "Some say John the Baptist; others say Elijah; and still others, Jeremiah or one of the prophets." "But what about you?" He asked. "Who do you say I am?" Simon Peter answered, "You are the Messiah, the Son of the living God." Jesus replied, "Blessed are you, Simon son of Jonah, for this was not revealed to you by flesh and blood, but by my Father in heaven. (Matthew 16:13-17)

Confirm the Truth

According to Matthew 16:13-17, who is Jesus Christ?

Understand the Truth

Notice the question Jesus asked His disciples. This is the world's most important question: "Who do you say Jesus is?" Many want to tell you that He was just a great religious teacher. But was He just that?

In his book *Mere Christianity*, the great 20th century thinker C. S. Lewis posed this solution:

> A man who was merely a man and said the sort of things Jesus said would not be a great moral teacher. He would either be a lunatic—on the level with a man who says he is a poached egg—or else he would be the Devil of Hell. You must make your choice. Either this man was, and is, the Son of God: or else a madman or something worse ...You can shut Him up for a fool, you can spit at Him and kill Him as a demon; or you can fall at His feet and call Him Lord and God. But let us not come up with any patronizing nonsense about His being a great human teacher. He has not left that open to us. He did not intend to.

Reflect and Respond

Who do you say that Jesus is and why?

WHAT OTHERS CLAIMED ABOUT JESUS

Read the Truth

In the beginning was the Word, and the Word was with God, and the Word was God, He was with God in the beginning. Through Him all things were made; without Him nothing was made that has been made. (John 1:1-3)

The Word became flesh and made His dwelling among us. We have seen His glory, the glory of the one and only Son, who came from the Father, full of grace and truth. (John 1:14)

Confirm the Truth

What claim did John (Jesus' disciple) make about Jesus ("the Word") in John 1:1-3?

What claim did John make about Jesus in John 1:14?

Understand the truth

Many modern skeptics say that Jesus never claimed to be God and that the writers of the New Testament never claimed that He was God. It is important that we test these statements against what the New Testament writers did claim about the deity of Jesus Christ.

John, the disciple (follower) of Jesus, wrote the gospel called by his name—*John.* In chapter 1, John claimed that Jesus was in the beginning, was with God, and was God. He also declared that Jesus was God's one and only Son who came to earth from heaven. John claimed that he was an eyewitness who could substantiate the claim that Jesus was God in human flesh.

Reflect and Respond

WHAT OTHERS CLAIMED ABOUT JESUS

Read the Truth

God has raised this Jesus to life, and we are all witnesses of it. Exalted to the right hand of God, He has received from the Father the promised Holy Spirit and has poured out what you now see and hear. For David did not ascend to heaven, and yet he said, "The LORD said to my Lord: 'Sit at my right hand until I make your enemies a footstool for your feet.'" Therefore let all Israel be assured of this: God has made this Jesus, whom you crucified, both Lord and Messiah." (Peter's sermon in Acts 2:32-36)

For we did not follow cleverly devised stories when we told you about the coming of our Lord Jesus Christ in power, but we were eyewitnesses of His majesty. He received honor and glory from God the Father when the voice came to Him from the Majestic Glory, saying, "This is my Son, whom I love; with Him I am well pleased." We ourselves heard this voice that came from heaven when we were with Him on the sacred mountain. (2 Peter 1:16-18)

Confirm the Truth

What claim did Peter make about Jesus in his sermon recorded in Acts 2:32-36?

What claim did Peter make about Jesus in 2 Peter 1:16-18?

Understand the truth

Continuing our look at what the New Testament writers claimed about the deity of Christ, we see that Peter, another one of Jesus' disciples, wrote and spoke about who he believed Jesus truly was. In his sermon recorded in Acts 2, Peter claimed that Jesus is at the right hand of God as both Lord and Christ. Peter declared that Jesus has poured out God's Holy Spirit on His followers as God promised He would do. In the second of the two letters he wrote that are preserved in the New Testament for us, Peter declared that he saw Jesus' majesty and heard the voice from heaven declaring Jesus to be God's Son. Both Peter and John were witnesses to the truths of these claims.

Reflect and Respond

WHAT OTHERS CLAIMED ABOUT JESUS

Read the Truth

In your relationships with one another, have the same mindset as Christ Jesus: Who, being in very nature God, did not consider equality with God something to be used to His own advantage; rather, He made himself nothing by taking the very nature of a servant, being made in human likeness. And being found in appearance as a man, He humbled Himself by becoming obedient to death—even death on a cross! Therefore God exalted Him to the highest place and gave Him the name that is above every name, that at the name of Jesus every knee should bow, in heaven and on earth and under the earth, and every tongue acknowledge that Jesus Christ is Lord, to the glory of God the Father. (Philippians 2:5-11)

Confirm the Truth

What claims did Paul make about Jesus Christ in Philippians 2:5-11?

Understand the Truth

Paul, who became one of Jesus' followers after the resurrection, preached the good news about Jesus in many cities and towns of the Roman Empire. Paul wrote 13 letters to churches and individuals that are preserved in the New Testament. In the letter to the Philippians, he declared with confidence that Jesus was in very nature God who took on human likeness in humility. God has given Him the name above every name. By this name, Jesus will be worshiped by every human being—living and dead—as Lord of all.

Reflect and Respond

WHAT OTHERS CLAIMED ABOUT JESUS

Read the Truth

The Son is the image of the invisible God, the firstborn over all creation. For in Him all things were created: things in heaven and on earth, visible and invisible, whether thrones or powers or rulers or authorities; all things have been created through Him and for Him. He is before all things, and in Him all things hold together. And He is the head of the body, the church; He is the beginning and the firstborn from among the dead, so that in everything He might have the supremacy. (Colossians 1:15-18)

For in Christ all the fullness of the Deity lives in bodily form, (Colossians 2:9)

Confirm the Truth

What claims did Paul make about Jesus Christ in Colossians 1:15-18?

What claim did Paul make about Jesus in Colossians 2:9?

Understand the Truth

In another one of Paul's letters, he declared that Jesus is the creator of everything and is, therefore, supreme over all creation. Jesus holds all things together. And Jesus is the supreme head of the entire church—all those who have believed in Him since His resurrection. There is no doubt in Paul's mind that Jesus Christ is the Son of God and equal to God Himself. In Colossians 2:9, Paul declares that in Christ, "all the fullness of God lives in bodily form." That's a pretty dramatic statement!

Reflect and Respond

WHAT OTHERS CLAIMED ABOUT JESUS

Read the Truth

In the past God spoke to our ancestors through the prophets at many times and in various ways, but in these last days He has spoken to us by His Son, whom He appointed heir of all things, and through whom also He made the universe. (Hebrews 1:1-2)

The Son is the radiance of God's glory and the exact representation of His being, sustaining all things by His powerful word. After He had provided purification for sins, He sat down at the right hand of the Majesty in heaven. So He became as much superior to the angels as the name He has inherited is superior to theirs. (Hebrews 1:3-4)

Confirm the Truth

What claim did the writer of Hebrews make about Jesus in Hebrews 1:1-2?

What claim did the writer of Hebrews make about Jesus in Hebrews 1:3-4?

Understand the Truth

We do not know who wrote the letter to the Hebrews. But that writer declared that through Jesus, God made the universe. The writer went on to describe Jesus, the Son of God, as the exact representation of God's being, sustainer of all things, sitting at the right hand of the Majesty in heaven and superior to the angels.

The New Testament writers are consistent in their claims about Jesus. They effectively declared that Jesus was truly God and not just a great teacher. If these writers knew that Jesus was not God and yet claimed that He was, you would conclude that they were liars, promoting a myth in order to somehow profit from it. But they did not do that. They declared what they had seen, heard, and known to be absolutely true.

Reflect and Respond

WHAT OTHERS CLAIMED ABOUT JESUS

Read the Truth

For what I received I passed on to you as of first importance: that Christ died for our sins according to the Scriptures, that He was buried, that He was raised on the third day according to the Scriptures, and that He appeared to Cephas, and then to the Twelve. After that, He appeared to more than five hundred of the brothers and sisters at the same time, most of whom are still living, though some have fallen asleep. Then He appeared to James, then to all the apostles, and last of all He appeared to me also, as to one abnormally born. (1 Corinthians 15:3-8)

Confirm the Truth

What does Paul claim about Jesus in 1 Corinthians 15:3-8?

Understand the Truth

From the beginning, the church has maintained that Jesus Christ, crucified and risen from the dead, is Savior and Lord of heaven and earth. Apart from His resurrection from the dead, historians have no feasible theory for the birth and progress of the Church. Paul confirms what was being taught everywhere about Jesus: that He died for our sins, that He was buried, and that He was raised from the dead—all according to what was promised in the Scriptures. His resurrected body was seen by more than 500 people and on at least 6 occasions. There were plenty of eyewitnesses to these truths.

There were, to be sure, ways of coping with the death of a teacher, or even a leader. ...The category of 'martyr' was available, within Judaism, for someone who stood up to pagans, and compromising no-better-than-pagans, and died still loyal to YHWH (the Hebrew name for God). The category of failed but still revered Messiah, however, did not exist. A Messiah who died at the hands of the pagans, instead of winning YHWH's battle against them, was a deceiver...Why then did people go on talking about Jesus of Nazareth, except as a remarkable but tragic memory? The obvious answer is the one given by all early Christians actually known to us. **Jesus was raised from the dead.... The resurrection, however we understand it, was the only reason why His life and words possessed any relevance two weeks, let alone two millennia, after His death.** (N.T. Wright, *Jesus and the Victory of God: Christian Origins and the Question of God, Volume 2*)

Reflect and Respond

WHAT OTHERS CLAIMED ABOUT JESUS

Read the Truth

Peter and John are arrested and brought before the Jewish religious governing body... But a Pharisee named Gamaliel, a teacher of the law, who was honored by all the people, stood up in the Sanhedrin and ordered that the men (Peter and John) be put outside for a little while. Then he addressed the Sanhedrin: "Men of Israel, consider carefully what you intend to do to these men. Some time ago Theudas appeared, claiming to be somebody, and about four hundred men rallied to him. He was killed, all his followers were dispersed, and it all came to nothing. After him, Judas the Galilean appeared in the days of the census and led a band of people in revolt. He too was killed, and all his followers were scattered. Therefore, in the present case I advise you: Leave these men alone! Let them go! For if their purpose or activity is of human origin, it will fail. But if it is from God, you will not be able to stop these men; you will only find yourselves fighting against God." (Acts 5:34-39)

Confirm the Truth

Regarding Peter and John, what advice is given to the skeptical religious leaders who lived after the time of Jesus (Acts 5:34-39)?

Understand the Truth

Wise Gamaliel recognized the power of God at work. He advised his peers to let Peter and John go. If this movement of claiming a resurrected Jesus is of human origin, it will fail. If it is of God, no one can stop it!

"The Christian church rests on the resurrection of its Founder. .... If Christ was raised from the dead, then all His other miracles are sure, and our faith is impregnable; if He was not raised, He died in vain, and our faith is vain. It was only His resurrection that made His death available for our atonement, justification, and salvation; without the resurrection, His death would be the grave of our hopes; we should be still unredeemed and under the power of our sins. A gospel of a dead Savior would be a contradiction and wretched delusion." (Philip Schaff, *History of the Christian Church, Volume 1*, p. 172)

Reflect and Respond

Do you believe that Jesus was raised from the dead according to the eyewitnesses who claimed this truth? How does your faith about this truth influence your life?

THE GOD YOU CAN KNOW

Read the Truth

Jesus answered, "I am the way and the truth and the life. No one comes to the Father except through me. If you really know me, you will know my Father as well. From now on, you do know Him and have seen Him." Philip said, "Lord, show us the Father and that will be enough for us." Jesus answered: "Don't you know me, Philip, even after I have been among you such a long time? Anyone who has seen me has seen the Father. How can you say, 'Show us the Father'? Don't you believe that I am in the Father, and that the Father is in me? The words I say to you I do not speak on my own authority. Rather, it is the Father, living in me, who is doing His work. (John 14:6-10)

Confirm the Truth

What does John 14:6-10 reveal about our being able to know God?

Understand the Truth

A relationship with God must be based on a true knowledge of the God who is. The Bible teaches that man can know truth about God. Jesus declared that one must go through Him to know God the Father. Jesus also demonstrated that seeing and knowing Him is the same as seeing and knowing God the Father. Both Jesus' words and His works come from God living in Jesus. The New Testament asserts that the invisible God can be known through His Son. Jesus is our Savior and our ultimate grace gift from God!

But you may be confused how Jesus could be God and the Spirit could be God and the Father could be God. Who is the one that is really God? The answer is all of them: three-in-one.

While confirming that there is only one true God, believers have worshiped Jesus Christ and have spoken of Him in terms appropriate only of deity from the earliest days of Christianity. The Holy Spirit is also known as deity. So the only conclusion is that the Bible clearly teaches three Divine Persons, each rightly called God, yet all the one and same God. The doctrine of the *Trinity* (or "Tri-unity," a man-made label) is a summary of the teachings of the Bible regarding the nature of God. We will cover this more in the next day's reading.

Reflect and Respond

DAY 24

THE GOD YOU CAN KNOW

Read the Truth

*Then Jesus came to them and said, "All authority in heaven and on earth has been given to me. Therefore go and make disciples of all nations, baptizing them in the name of the **Father** and of the **Son** and of the **Holy Spirit**, and teaching them to obey everything I have commanded you. And surely I am with you always, to the very end of the age." (Matthew 28:18-20)*

*May the grace of the **Lord Jesus Christ**, and the love of **God**, and the fellowship of the **Holy Spirit** be with you all. (2 Corinthians 13:14)*

*Peter, an apostle of Jesus Christ, To God's elect, exiles scattered throughout the provinces of Pontus, Galatia, Cappadocia, Asia and Bithynia, who have been chosen according to the foreknowledge of **God the Father**, through the sanctifying work of the **Spirit**, to be obedient to **Jesus Christ** and sprinkled with His blood: Grace and peace be yours in abundance. (1 Peter 1:1-2)*

*When all the people were being baptized, **Jesus** was baptized too. And as He was praying, heaven was opened and the **Holy Spirit** descended on Him in bodily form like a dove. And a voice came from heaven: "You are **my Son**, whom I love; with you I am well pleased." (Luke 3:21-22)*

Confirm the Truth

In each of the verses you just read, the three representations of the one true God are mentioned together. Fill in the blanks below:

...baptizing them in the name of the _____ and of the _____ and of

the _____ (Matthew 28:18-20)

May the grace of the _____, and the love of

_____, and the fellowship of the _____ be with you all. (2

Corinthians 13:14)

...who have been chosen according to the foreknowledge of _____,

through the sanctifying work of the _____, to be obedient to _____ (1

Peter 1:1-2)

... _____ was baptized too. And as He was praying, heaven was opened and the

_____ descended on Him in bodily form like a dove. And a voice came from heaven:

"You are _____, whom I love... (Luke 3:21-22)

Understand the Truth

The doctrine of the Trinity ("Tri-unity") was formulated by the church after many years of reflecting on the biblical data and after rejecting many inadequate theories. The Bible teaches monotheism—the insistence that there is only one true God (Exodus 20:2-3; Isaiah 42:8; 45:5). *Without denying biblical monotheism*, the apostles and early church worshiped Jesus Christ and

34

honored three Persons as God: the Father, the Son, and the Holy Spirit (Matthew 28:18-20; 2 Corinthians 13:14). Because of this, outsiders accused the church of falling into either *polytheism* (belief in more than one God) or *idolatry* (improperly worshiping someone as God - in this case, Jesus).

So church leaders gathered in Nicene (modern Turkey) to verbalize what God revealed about Himself: one in essence, three in persons. They wrote what is known as the Nicene Creed.

> I believe in one God the Father Almighty, maker of heaven and earth, and of all things visible and invisible; and in one Lord Jesus Christ, the only-begotten Son of God, begotten of His Father before all worlds, God of God, Light of Light, very God of very God, begotten, not made, being of one substance with the Father, by whom all things were made; Who for us men and for our salvation came down from heaven and was incarnate by the Holy Spirit of the Virgin Mary...And I believe in the Holy Spirit the Lord and giver of life, who proceeds from the Father and the Son, who with the Father and the Son together is worshiped and glorified... (*Nicene Creed*, AD 325)

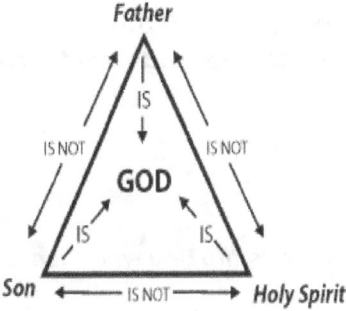

The doctrine of the Trinity was defined after careful Bible study and debate. Since the earliest century, it has stood as an accurate representation of the Bible's teaching: **God is one in essence, three in Person.** The diagram at right is an attempt to picture this.

Reflect and Respond

35

THE GOD YOU CAN KNOW

Read the Truth

This is good, and pleases God our Savior, who wants all people to be saved and to come to a knowledge of the truth. For there is one God and one mediator between God and mankind, the man Christ Jesus, who gave Himself as a ransom for all people. This has now been witnessed to at the proper time. (1 Timothy 2:3-6)

Confirm the Truth

What does God want for all men?

Who is the one who mediates between God and humanity?

Why is He the mediator?

Understand the Truth

God invites all men into a personal relationship with Himself through faith in His Son Jesus Christ. If Jesus Christ is who He claimed to be, then *knowing Him* is the single most important issue in all of life. You can have a personal relationship with God through faith in his Son Jesus Christ.

> Today, all sorts of subjects are eagerly pursued; but the knowledge of God is neglected...Yet to know God is man's chief end, and justifies his existence. Even if a hundred lives were ours, this one aim would be sufficient for them all. (John Calvin)

Reflect and Respond

If knowing Him is the most important issue in all of life, what choice(s) do you need to make in order to grow in the process of knowing Him?

part 3

GRACE-COVERED SIN

The next day John saw Jesus coming toward him and said, "Look, the Lamb of God, who takes away the sin of the world!" (John 1:29)

THE CROSS: GOD'S SOLUTION TO THE SIN DISEASE

Read the Truth

"The next day John saw Jesus coming toward him and said, 'Look, the Lamb of God, who takes away the sin of the world!'" (John 1:29)

Confirm the Truth

What did John the Baptist declare about Jesus?

Understand the Truth

The ultimate grace gift came—Jesus Christ. But why did He come? What was His purpose? From the time sin entered into the relationship of humans with their Creator God, the one question that continually demands an answer is, "How can guilty sinful people be made right in the eyes of a holy God?" John declared that God was sending an answer to this question in Jesus (John 1:29).

Humanity's spiritual problem can be compared to death caused by a fatal disease: (1) Sin ("the disease" Romans 3:23—all sinned) and (2) Death ("result of the disease" Romans 6:23—wages of sin). Our twofold problem demanded a twofold solution:

1) For our sin disease, people need forgiveness and righteousness. *Answer: Christ's **death** on the cross*. We can now be cured of the disease.

2) For our state of death, people need regeneration (the restoration of **life**). *Answer: Christ's **resurrection***. We can now be given life that is forever.

The Gospel message included the answer to both spiritual problems. The following quote by a 20th century Bible teacher captures the gospel message in a nutshell.

Jesus Christ **laid down** His life **for** you so that He could **give** His life **to** you so that He could **live** His life **through** you. (Ian Thomas, *The Saving Life of Christ*)

Reflect and Respond

THE CROSS: GOD'S SOLUTION TO THE SIN DISEASE

Read the Truth

This is the message we have heard from Him and declare to you: God is light; in Him there is no darkness at all. (1 John 1:5)

The heart is deceitful above all things and beyond cure. Who can understand it? (Jeremiah 17:9)

Confirm the Truth

What does John (Jesus' disciple) declare about God in 1 John 1:5?

What does God declare through the Old Testament prophet Jeremiah about the human heart (Jeremiah 17:9)?

Understand the Truth

Our God is a holy God, meaning He is completely separated from anything that is sinful or evil. There is no sin in Him at all. As John writes, "God is light; in Him there is no darkness at all." God is perfect. It is a unique part of His character—who He is.

Humans are not holy. Jeremiah describes the human heart as being deceitful above all things and beyond cure. Some translations use the phrase "desperately wicked" to describe human sickness. This is a part of our character—a part of every human. Thus, there is a gap between God's holiness and human sinfulness, or "sickness." Sin is a disease beyond human cure.

Reflect and Respond

THE CROSS: GOD'S SOLUTION TO THE SIN DISEASE

Read the Truth

The wrath of God is being revealed from heaven against all the godlessness and wickedness of people, who suppress the truth by their wickedness, since what may be known about God is plain to them, because God has made it plain to them. For since the creation of the world God's invisible qualities—His eternal power and divine nature—have been clearly seen, being understood from what has been made, so that people are without excuse. For although they knew God, they neither glorified Him as God nor gave thanks to Him, but their thinking became futile and their foolish hearts were darkened. Although they claimed to be wise, they became fools and exchanged the glory of the immortal God for images made to look like a mortal human being and birds and animals and reptiles. (Romans 1:18-23)

What shall we conclude then? Do we have any advantage? Not at all! For we have already made the charge that Jews and Gentiles alike are all under the power of sin. As it is written: "There is no one righteous, not even one; there is no one who understands; there is no one who seeks God. All have turned away, they have together become worthless; there is no one who does good, not even one." (Romans 3:9-12)

Confirm the Truth

What does Paul reveal about human sickness in Romans 1:18-23?

What does Paul reveal about human sickness in Romans 3:9-12?

Understand the Truth

Paul's description of godless or wicked people is very telling. God's invisible qualities—His eternal power and divine nature—have been clearly seen, being understood from what has been made, so that people are without excuse. Yet, people willingly suppress the truth and exchange the truth about God for a lie. Jews or non-Jews—all experience the human sin disease. All are sinful. None do good on their own. No one is righteous apart from God. Such sickness leads to destructive behavior. And it leads to death and separation from a holy God. Not a pretty picture but yet a reality we must all face.

Reflect and Respond

THE CROSS: GOD'S SOLUTION TO THE SIN DISEASE

Read the Truth

By the sweat of your brow you will eat your food until you return to the ground, since from it you were taken;
for dust you are and to dust you will return. (Genesis 3:19)

The wrath of God is being revealed from heaven against all the godlessness and wickedness of people, who suppress the truth by their wickedness... (Romans 1:18)

Therefore, just as sin entered the world through one man, and death through sin, and in this way death came to all people, because all sinned... (Romans 5:12)

Confirm the Truth

What is God's pronouncement of judgment on human sinfulness in Genesis 3:19?

What is God's response to human sinfulness in Romans 1:18?

What is God's pronouncement of judgment on human sinfulness in Romans 5:12?

Understand the Truth

The death mentioned in the three verses you just read refers to both physical death and spiritual separation from God. Both are the end result of sin's effect on all life. God's response to all evil and sin is righteous, holy wrath (Romans 1:18). We must not project our experience with human anger onto God and assume that "His is the same, only bigger." God's wrath is not a *mood* or a fit of *temper.* God's disposition toward sin and evil is as constant and unrelenting as His love and goodness. He hates and rejects evil in a perfect and holy anger. He will never bend nor compromise with it. His own nature demands that He judge it through action. A Christian writer from the 20th century described it this way:

> Since God's first concern for His universe is its moral health, that is, its holiness, whatever is contrary to this is necessarily under His eternal displeasure. Wherever the holiness of God confronts unholiness there is conflict: This conflict arises from the irreconcilable natures of holiness and sin.

41

God's attitude and action in the conflict are His anger. **To preserve His creation God must destroy whatever would destroy it.** When He arises to put down destruction and save the world from irreparable moral collapse He is said to be angry. Every wrathful judgment of God in the history of the world has been a holy act of preservation. (A.W. Tozer, *The Knowledge of the Holy*, p. 106)

Let's put this in everyday terms that you and I can understand. How much do you hate germs like the flu virus infiltrating your home? Do you use a disinfectant to clean with gusto and keep your family from getting sick? I don't know about you, but my disposition toward the flu virus or a stomach virus is wrath. It is pollution of my home. Another example is an ant infestation in your home. You do not invite them in and just ignore their presence while they take over your kitchen or bedroom, do you? I bet you do whatever you can to attack their presence and restore your home to a safe environment for your family. When I spray ant killer where I've seen ants crawling in my kitchen, I am expressing wrath against their destruction of my safe home environment.

God's wrath is far more serious, of course. Sin is much more awful with far more destructive consequences than the flu virus or ants. But you get the idea.

Reflect and Respond

42

THE CROSS: GOD'S SOLUTION TO THE SIN DISEASE

Read the Truth

The Lord God made garments of skin for Adam and his wife and clothed them. (Genesis 3:21)

Tell the whole community of Israel that on the tenth day of this month each man is to take a lamb for his family, one for each household... Take care of them until the fourteenth day of the month, when all the members of the community of Israel must slaughter them at twilight. Then they are to take some of the blood and put it on the sides and tops of the doorframes of the houses where they eat the lamb... The blood will be a sign for you on the houses where you are, and when I see the blood, I will pass over you. No destructive plague will touch you when I strike Egypt. (Exodus 12:3, 6-7, 13)

This is how Aaron is to enter the Most Holy Place: He must first bring a young bull for a sin offering and a ram for a burnt offering. He is to put on the sacred linen tunic, with linen undergarments next to his body; he is to tie the linen sash around him and put on the linen turban. These are sacred garments; so he must bathe himself with water before he puts them on. From the Israelite community he is to take two male goats for a sin offering and a ram for a burnt offering. (Leviticus 16:3-5)

Confirm the Truth

Because God is holy, sin must be judged. God prescribed a substitute to pay the penalty for human sin.

What substitute paid the penalty for human sin in Genesis 3:21?

What substitute paid the price to protect Israel in Exodus 12:3, 5-7, 12-13?

What substitutes paid the penalty for human sin in Leviticus 16:3-5?

Understand the Truth

Animals died to provide skin garments to cover Adam and Eve. A lamb died to provide blood to cover the doorframes to protect the Israelites from the plague. A young bull and two male goats died as sin offerings to pay the penalty for the priest's sins as well as for those of the community of Israel.

43

The purposes of the animal sacrifices prescribed in the Old Testament were:

1) To teach the seriousness of sin.

2) To teach that God is forgiving, but that forgiveness comes *only at a price,* through the death of an innocent substitute.

3) To provide a place for a person to transfer guilt and receive temporary forgiveness.

4) To point symbolically to Christ's ultimate sacrifice.

The death of the animal was a sad and ugly thing just as sin is a sad and ugly thing. But the innocent animal's sacrifice provided forgiveness for human sin and opened the way for a person to have a relationship with a holy God.

Reflect and Respond

THE CROSS: GOD'S SOLUTION TO THE SIN DISEASE

Read the Truth

Now if you as a community unintentionally fail to keep any of these commands the LORD gave Moses...and if this is done unintentionally without the community being aware of it, then the whole community is to offer a young bull for a burnt offering as an aroma pleasing to the LORD ... and a male goat for a sin offering. The priest is to make atonement for the whole Israelite community, and they will be forgiven, for it was not intentional and they have presented to the LORD for their wrong a food offering and a sin offering. ... But if just one person sins unintentionally, that person must bring a year-old female goat for a sin offering. The priest is to make atonement before the LORD for the one who erred by sinning unintentionally, and when atonement has been made, that person will be forgiven. One and the same law applies to everyone who sins unintentionally, whether a native-born Israelite or a foreigner residing among you. But anyone who sins defiantly, whether native-born or foreigner, blasphemes the LORD and must be cut off from the people of Israel. Because they have despised the Lord's word and broken His commands, they must surely be cut off; their guilt remains on them. (Numbers 15:22-31)

Confirm the Truth

What prescribed sacrifices covered unintentional sin (Number 15:22-31)?

If someone sinned intentionally ("defiantly"), then what happened?

Understand the Truth

People in Old Testament times were accepted by God and received eternal life in the same way as we are today—by faith in the merciful grace of God (though the *content* of their knowledge was different). For daily living, however, forgiveness was taught and dispensed differently under the Law. Forgiveness under the Law came through "atonement," literally, a "covering." Guilt was "covered" for some undetermined time. Forgiveness under the Law was dispensed in a piecemeal fashion. It could be obtained "up to date" but not given in advance, and it was temporary and limited.

Forgiveness for "unintentional" sins was obtained through prescribed sacrifices. For anyone who sinned defiantly (with daring or bold resistance to authority), there was no forgiveness through the Law apart from the once per year removal on the Day of Atonement. Those who deliberately sinned must throw themselves on the mercy of God. Forgiveness was not automatic! Heart attitudes were measured. God measured the heart attitudes and responded to faith with forgiveness (David in 2 Samuel 12:13).

Reflect and Respond

THE CROSS: GOD'S SOLUTION TO THE SIN DISEASE

Read the Truth

For I desire mercy, not sacrifice, and acknowledgment of God rather than burnt offerings. (Hosea 6:6)

With what shall I come before the LORD and bow down before the exalted God? Shall I come before Him with burnt offerings, with calves a year old? Will the LORD be pleased with thousands of rams, with ten thousand rivers of olive oil? Shall I offer my firstborn for my transgression, the fruit of my body for the sin of my soul? He has shown you, O mortal, what is good. And what does the LORD require of you? To act justly and to love mercy and to walk humbly with your God. (Micah 6:6-8)

The law is only a shadow of the good things that are coming—not the realities themselves. For this reason it can never, by the same sacrifices repeated endlessly year after year, make perfect those who draw near to worship. Otherwise, would they not have stopped being offered? For the worshipers would have been cleansed once for all, and would no longer have felt guilty for their sins. But those sacrifices are an annual reminder of sins. It is impossible for the blood of bulls and goats to take away sins. (Hebrews 10:1-4)

Confirm the Truth

What does God say about His desire regarding the human heart in Hosea 6:6?

What does God say about His desire regarding the human heart in Micah 6:6-8?

According to Hebrews 10:1-4, why was forgiveness through the Law ultimately inadequate?

Understand the Truth

As the prophet Hosea declared, God desires both men and women to love mercy and to acknowledge Him. Sacrifices apart from faithfulness to the Lord's will are wholly unacceptable to Him. The prophet Micah wrote that God desires His people to act justly, love mercy and walk humbly before Him. Righteous hearts and righteous behavior are better than sacrifices. God wants obedience, not compliance.

Compliance is an act of yielding to a wish, request or demand of someone in authority. It is basically just keeping the rules. Obedience is an act of submission to the authority, springing from commitment and trust. God has always wanted obedient hearts more than compliance, which is just following the rules without the heart being touched.

Adding to the hard-heartedness associated with the sacrifices is the truth that forgiveness through the Mosaic Law was ultimately inadequate anyway. The sacrifices had to be repeated annually. The sacrifices could not make perfect those who were even doing it. The sacrifices could not cleanse once for all. The sacrifices could not take away guilt. God had a solution planned that would be so much better!

Reflect and Respond

CHRIST'S FINISHED WORK ON THE CROSS

Read the Truth

He then began to teach them that the Son of Man must suffer many things and be rejected by the elders, the chief priests and the teachers of the law, and that He must be killed and after three days rise again. (Mark 8:31)

"For even the Son of Man did not come to be served, but to serve, and to give His life as a ransom for many." (Mark 10:45)

He said to them, "How foolish you are, and how slow to believe all that the prophets have spoken! Did not the Messiah have to suffer these things and then enter His glory?" And beginning with Moses and all the Prophets, He explained to them what was said in all the Scriptures concerning Himself. (Luke 24:25-27)

He said to them, "This is what I told you while I was still with you: Everything must be fulfilled that is written about me in the Law of Moses, the Prophets and the Psalms." Then He opened their minds so they could understand the Scriptures. He told them, "This is what is written: The Messiah will suffer and rise from the dead on the third day, and repentance for the forgiveness of sins will be preached in His name to all nations, beginning at Jerusalem. (Luke 24:44-47)

Confirm the Truth

What did Jesus teach His disciples about His purpose in Mark 8:31?

What else did Jesus remind His followers about His purpose in Mark 10:45?

How did Jesus remind His followers about His purpose in Luke 24:25-27?

What did Jesus remind His disciples about His purpose in Luke 24:44-47?

Understand the Truth

In Mark 8:31, Jesus taught that He must suffer, be rejected by the Jewish religious leaders, and be killed. But He would rise again on the third day. His purpose was to serve and give His life as a ransom for many (Mark 10:45). Speaking to His disciples, Jesus reminded them what the Scriptures had declared all along that He would suffer, then enter His glory. Repentance and forgiveness of sins will be preached in His name to all nations.

Jesus understood His purpose—to give His life for all humanity. This was no surprise to Him or to God the Father who sent Him. It was God's plan all along. Jesus would accomplish His purpose through His death and resurrection.

Reflect and Respond

CHRIST'S FINISHED WORK ON THE CROSS

Read the Truth

He Himself bore our sin in His body on the cross, so that we might die to sins and live for righteousness; by His wounds you have been healed. (1 Peter 2:24)

For Christ also suffered once for sins, the righteous for the unrighteous, to bring you to God. He was put to death in the body but made alive in the Spirit. (1 Peter 3:18)

You see, at just the right time, when we were still powerless, Christ died for the ungodly. Very rarely will anyone die for a righteous person, though for a good person someone might possibly dare to die. But God demonstrates His own love for us in this: While we were still sinners, Christ died for us. (Romans 5:6-8)

Confirm the Truth

What did Peter emphasize about Jesus' death in 1 Peter 2:24?

What did Peter emphasize about Jesus' death in 1 Peter 3:18?

What did Paul emphasize about Jesus' death in Romans 5:6-8?

Understand the Truth

As Peter wrote, Jesus bore our sins in His own body so that we might die to sin and live for righteousness. What a change in life strategy for us! By His wounds, we are healed of our sin disease and brought near to God. Jesus does that for everyone who believes in Him. And Paul wrote that God demonstrated His love for us in that while we were still sinners, Jesus died for us. Isn't that act of love for ungodly humans such an amazing thing?!

Reflect and Respond

CHRIST'S FINISHED WORK ON THE CROSS

Read the Truth

But when Christ came as high priest of the good things that are now already here, He went through the greater and more perfect tabernacle that is not made with human hands, that is to say, is not a part of this creation. He did not enter by means of the blood of goats and calves; but He entered the Most Holy Place once for all by His own blood, thus obtaining eternal redemption. The blood of goats and bulls and the ashes of a heifer sprinkled on those who are ceremonially unclean sanctify them so that they are outwardly clean. How much more, then, will the blood of Christ, who through the eternal Spirit offered Himself unblemished to God, cleanse our consciences from acts that lead to death, so that we may serve the living God! For this reason Christ is the mediator of a new covenant, that those who are called may receive the promised eternal inheritance—now that He has died as a ransom to set them free from the sins committed under the first covenant. (Hebrews 9:11-15)

Day after day every priest stands and performs his religious duties; again and again he offers the same sacrifices, which can never take away sins. But when this priest [Jesus] had offered for all time one sacrifice for sins, He sat down at the right hand of God, and since that time He waits for His enemies to be made His footstool. For by one sacrifice He has made perfect forever those who are being made holy. (Hebrews 10:11-14)

Confirm the Truth

How is Christ's offering better than the old system (Hebrews 9:11-15)?

How is Christ's work better than the old system (Hebrews 10:11-14)?

Understand the Truth

When Jesus said, "It is finished" in John 19:30, He meant just that. Finished. Complete. Done once for all. The writer of Hebrews confirmed this to be true. Whereas the sacrifices made under the Old Testament law were not able to clear the conscience of the worshiper, the blood of Christ cleanses our consciences so we may freely and joyfully serve God. The sacrifices could never take away sins, only cover them. Christ's sacrifice, however, has not only taken away the sins but also made perfect forever those who are being made holy—all believers.

Reflect and Respond

51

CHRIST'S FINISHED WORK ON THE CROSS

Read the Truth

At that moment the curtain of the temple was torn in two from top to bottom. (Matthew 27:51)

But only the high priest entered the inner room [the Most Holy Place], and that only once a year, and never without blood, which he offered for himself and for the sins the people had committed in ignorance. (Hebrews 9:7)

Therefore, brothers and sisters, since we have confidence to enter the Most Holy Place by the blood of Jesus, by a new and living way opened for us through the curtain, that is, His body, and since we have a great priest over the house of God, let us draw near to God with a sincere heart and with the full assurance that faith brings, having our hearts sprinkled to cleanse us from a guilty conscience and having our bodies washed with pure water. (Hebrews 10:19-22)

Confirm the Truth

What happened in Matthew 27:51?

Before this, who alone could enter the Most Holy Place and with what?

Now, who can enter the Most Holy Place (God's presence) because of Jesus' blood (Hebrews 9:7 and 10:19-22)?

What is the benefit to you in doing so?

Understand the Truth

There was a curtain in the temple that separated the main room of the temple from the Most Holy Place representing God's presence with His people. When Jesus died on the cross, this curtain was torn from top to bottom. God did this. Now we can enter the Most Holy Place (God's

presence) with confidence by the blood of Jesus. We no longer rely on a High Priest going in once a year to represent us before God. Jesus is our High Priest, His body is the torn curtain, and we can draw near to God with full assurance of already being cleansed of all sin. What a marvelous opportunity!

> God tore the curtain, for when the Lord Jesus Christ 'became sin for us,' and purchased our salvation by his own blood, the regulations of the old covenant were rendered null and void. Never again would God require the blood of a bull, a goat or a lamb. The priesthood was now defunct, the temple redundant and the law abolished. (Charles Price, *Alive in Christ,* p. 80)

Our disease problem is cured. Through His sacrifice, Christ has done all that needs to be done to reconcile guilty people to a holy God. This is the meaning of the phrase, *"justification by faith."* For any person, all that is required to benefit from what Jesus accomplished is to believe or trust in Him.

Justification is God's act as Judge, where He declares a guilty sinner to be totally righteous on the basis of Christ's finished work on the cross and that person's faith in Christ. Justification involves both a negative and positive aspect. Negatively, justification is the removal of guilt from the offender ("forgiveness"). Positively, justification is the addition of righteousness to the one who believes (Romans 5:17). This is called the "Great Exchange." Paul describes it clearly in 2 Corinthians,

> God made Him who had no sin to be sin for us, so that in Him we might become the righteousness of God. (2 Corinthians 5:21)

Reflect and Respond

DAY 37

CHRIST'S FINISHED WORK ON THE CROSS

Read the Truth

Whoever believes in the Son of God accepts this testimony. Whoever does not believe God has made Him out to be a liar, because they have not believed the testimony God has given about His Son. And this is the testimony: God has given us eternal life, and this life is in His Son. Whoever has the Son has life; whoever does not have the Son of God does not have life. I write these things to you who believe in the name of the Son of God so that you may know that you have eternal life. (1 John 5:10-13)

Confirm the Truth

According to 1 John 5:10-13, what can you know for sure?

Why can you know this for sure?

Understand the Truth

We can know for sure that God has given us eternal life through faith (belief) in His Son. We have it already. Assurance of salvation can be known and experienced by (1) clearly understanding the gospel, and (2) trusting God's promises in Jesus Christ. Assurance is not confidence in our own ability to hold on to Christ but confidence in *Him* and His promises to hold on to us!

Reflect and Respond

JUSTIFICATION BY FAITH ALONE

Read the Truth

Now we know that whatever the law says, it says to those who are under the law, so that every mouth may be silenced and the whole world held accountable to God. Therefore no one will be declared righteous in God's sight by the works of the law; rather, through the law we become conscious of our sin. But now apart from the law the righteousness of God has been made known, to which the Law and the Prophets testify. This righteousness is given through faith in Jesus Christ to all who believe. There is no difference between Jew and Gentile, for all have sinned and fall short of the glory of God, and all are justified freely by His grace through the redemption that came by Christ Jesus. (Romans 3:19-24)

God presented Christ as a sacrifice of atonement, through the shedding of His blood—to be received by faith. He did this to demonstrate His righteousness, because in His forbearance He had left the sins committed beforehand unpunished—He did it to demonstrate His righteousness at the present time, so as to be just and the one who justifies those who have faith in Jesus. Where, then, is boasting? It is excluded. Because of what law? The law that requires works? No, because of the law that requires faith. For we maintain that a person is justified by faith apart from the works of the law. (Romans 3:25-28)

Therefore, since we have been justified through faith, we have peace with God through our Lord Jesus Christ, through whom we have gained access by faith into this grace in which we now stand. And we boast in the hope of the glory of God. (Romans 5:1-2)

Confirm the Truth

Romans 3:19-28 is often called "the heart of the Bible." According to Romans 3:19-24, what is declared about the source of your justification?

What is declared in Romans 3:25-28 about the source of your justification?

What does Romans 5:1-2 say about how you are justified before God?

Understand the Truth

As Paul stated so clearly in Romans 3, we all are justified freely by His grace through the redemption that came by Jesus Christ. This comes to us by faith apart from any works that we do. This is true for all who believe (verse 22). It is a gift of God. He does this to exclude all boasting in our own efforts.

We receive justification (being declared not guilty of sin) by faith in Jesus Christ. Romans 5:1-2 declares that we have been justified through faith. Through Christ, we have gained access by faith into His grace in which we now stand.

Reflect and Respond

DAY 39

JUSTIFICATION BY FAITH ALONE

Read the Truth

For it is by grace you have been saved, through faith—and this is not from yourselves, it is the gift of God—not by works, so that no one can boast. (Ephesians 2:8-9)

Confirm the Truth

What does Ephesians 2:8-9 teach about your salvation?

Understand the Truth

Our salvation comes through faith as a gift of God, not by our works. It is a result of God's grace to us. Remember that grace is "unmerited favor." Consider the benefits of knowing that both your salvation and your justification ("not guilty" standing before God) are by faith alone rather than through any works you must do to earn God's forgiveness. As a result, you can enjoy living in the confidence of your relationship with God and your eternal destiny. You can experience true freedom from having to pay penance (make amends) to God because of your sin. Your heart can feel true gratefulness for what God has done for you. ☺

> Do you want to give up the guilt? Or do you prefer to hang onto it like an heirloom? Forgetting you've been cleansed from past sins makes you nearsighted and blind and keeps you from developing maturity in Christ (2 Peter 1:9). A failure to recognize and trust that the sin issue between you and God is over will effectively stop your spiritual growth in Christ...We can become totally preoccupied with the thing that God is *finished* dealing with—sin—that we neglect what God is trying to do with us *today*— teach us about life! (Bob George, *Classic Christianity*, p. 60)

Reflect and Respond

JUSTIFICATION BY FAITH ALONE

Read the Truth

Read this old Irish hymn by Charities Lees Smith written in 1863 under the name "The Advocate." It is now called "Before the Throne of God Above" and is a beautiful illustration of what Christ has done for you.

Before the throne of God above, I have a strong and perfect plea.
A great high Priest whose Name is Love, whoever lives and pleads for me.
My name is graven on His hands, my name is written on His heart.
I know that while in heaven He stands, no tongue can bid me to depart. No tongue can bid me to depart.

When Satan tempts me to despair and tells me of the guilt within.
Upward I look and see Him there who made an end to all my sin.
Because the sinless Savior died, my sinful soul is counted free.
For God the just is satisfied to look on Him and pardon me. To look on Him and pardon me.

Behold Him there the risen Lamb, my perfect spotless righteousness. The great unchangeable I am the King of glory and of grace. One with Himself I cannot die; my soul is purchased by His blood. My life is hid with Christ on high with Christ my Savior and my God! With Christ my Savior and my God!

Reflect and Respond

Reflect on the words to the song above. Respond in any way you choose (journaling, prayer, poem, art, song) to illustrate your thanks to God for ending the sacrificial system and completely forgiving you by your faith in Christ alone.

part 4

GRACE TRIUMPHANT

When you were dead in your sins and in the uncircumcision of your flesh, God made you alive with Christ. He forgave us all our sins, having canceled the charge of our legal indebtedness, which stood against us and condemned us; He has taken it away, nailing it to the cross. And having disarmed the powers and authorities, He made a public spectacle of them, triumphing over them by the cross.
(Colossians 2:13-15)

ANNOUNCEMENT TO THE WORLD: IT IS FINISHED!

Read the Truth

Therefore, my brothers, I want you to know that through Jesus the forgiveness of sins is proclaimed to you. Through Him everyone who believes is justified from everything you could not be justified from by the Law of Moses. (Acts 13:38-39)

For God so loved the world that He gave His one and only Son, that whoever believes in Him shall not perish but have eternal life. For God did not send His Son into the world to condemn the world, but to save the world through Him. Whoever believes in Him is not condemned, but whoever does not believe stands condemned already because they have not believed in the name of God's one and only Son. (John 3:16-18)

Confirm the Truth

What truth did Paul declare in Acts 13:38-39?

What truth is given about "whoever believes in Him" (John 3:16-18)?

What truth is given about those who do not believe in Him (John 3:16-18)?

Understand the Truth

The gospel is an announcement to the world of an accomplished fact. What God set out to do for humans, He accomplished. Salvation is available on the basis of a single condition: faith (or "belief"). Belief is not just intellectual assent that something might be true. Belief is a commitment of the will. It is the difference between walking alongside a pool of water (seeing it is there) and floating on the water (experiencing the water personally). God acted; we respond to His action by saying yes and jumping into the new life God has for us. Those who respond with faith in Jesus Christ, God's Son, receive a firm assurance of security (1 John 5:13), a secure new identity in Christ (2 Corinthians 5:17), and a true knowledge of God as seen through all that He has done through Christ's finished work on the cross.

Reflect and Respond

CHRIST'S FINISHED WORK ON THE CROSS

Six terms describe how our relationship with God is changed because of our faith in Jesus Christ—PROPITIATION, RECONCILIATION, REDEMPTION, FORGIVENESS, JUSTIFICATION, and SANCTIFICATION. These 6 relationship changes are the direct result of **Christ's finished work on the cross** so they are often called "words of the cross." We will cover them one at a time.

Word of the Cross #1 Propitiation: "God's holy wrath is fully satisfied"

Propitiation (prō-ˌpi-shē-ˈā-shən) is an old word we do not use in our daily vocabulary. Using a dictionary for its verb form *propitiate*, you would see that it means, "to conciliate or appease." Basically, it means to satisfy or appease someone in order to win favor from him/her. That implies you have done something to lose their favor, usually something incurring anger.

You can probably recall a time when you incurred the anger of someone you love and needed to make some kind of restitution to "appease" their anger. The act of appeasement leads to that person now being satisfied because restitution has been made. So the relationship can be restored. That is the basis for propitiation.

Read the Truth

*[Christ] whom God displayed publicly as a **propitiation** in His blood through faith. This was to demonstrate His righteousness, because in the forbearance of God He passed over the sins previously committed; (Romans 3:25, NASV)*

*In this is love, not that we loved God, but that He loved us and sent His Son to be the **propitiation** for our sins. Beloved, if God so loved us, we also ought to love one another. (1 John 4:10, NASV)*

Confirm the Truth

According to Romans 3:25, God displayed Christ publicly as what?

Because of the forbearance of God, what could He now do for us (Romans 3:25)?

Because of God's love, what did He do for us (1 John 4:10)?

61

Understand the Truth

God presented Christ as a sacrifice of propitiation for our sins. Some translations use the words "sacrifice of atonement" or "atoning sacrifice" instead. The concept of God's satisfaction is the same.

Biblical *propitiation* represents an important change in our relationship with God. It is often associated with God's mercy toward us. Mercy is commonly defined as "not getting what we deserve." Our problem before Christ: God's righteous anger toward human sin. Remember that God's wrath is an action against sin to preserve His creation, not a mood or fit of temper. Without appeasement, all people are justly destined for eternal punishment. But God, out of His great mercy, provided a way for His anger against human sin to be satisfied through blood sacrifice on the Day of Atonement in the Old Testament (Leviticus 16) and finally through Jesus' sacrificial death on the cross.

In the New Testament, the same word used to describe God's "satisfaction" with Jesus' shed blood also describes the top surface of the Ark of the Covenant in the Holy of Holies. This surface was called the "atonement cover" or the "mercy seat" in Hebrews 9:5, depending on the translation. The mercy seat was sprinkled with the blood of the sacrifice (a perfect lamb) on the annual Day of Atonement. By this ceremony, God's anger at sin was appeased, and the people's sins were forgiven up to that point. Jesus' death on the cross provided the permanent way that God's anger against human sin was appeased. The New Testament writers teach that Jesus' **sacrifice of atonement** fully satisfied God's righteous anger against human sin for those who trust in Him.

Reflect and Respond

DAY 43

CHRIST'S FINISHED WORK ON THE CROSS

Word of the Cross #1 PROPITIATION: "God's holy wrath is fully satisfied"

Read the Truth

*And He Himself is the **propitiation** for our sins; and not for ours only, but also for those of the whole world. (1 John 2:2, NASV)*

Confirm the Truth

According to 1 John 2:2, to whom does God's offer of mercy extend?

Understand the Truth

Because Jesus Christ has endured in our place the full wrath of God for our sins, God is able to extend mercy without compromise with evil. His holiness has been fully satisfied with the offering of Jesus Christ. The payment has been made for the whole world. God's mercy extends to the whole world. But it must be individually acknowledged. God acted. The response He expects is belief in His Son. Why would anyone not jump at the opportunity to take this wonderful offer?!

You can dwell on the FACT that God's anger at human sin was fully satisfied by Jesus' finished work on the cross. The second verse of the beautiful song, *In Christ Alone*, expresses this:

> In Christ alone, who took on flesh, fullness of God in helpless babe!
> This gift of love and righteousness scorned by the ones He came to save.
> 'Til on that cross as Jesus died, **the wrath of God was satisfied.**
> For every sin on Him was laid; here in the death of Christ I live. (Stuart Townend)

Reflect and Respond

You CAN know and live with confidence that God is no longer angry at your sin because you believe in His Son. He is no longer angry with you.

How does that make you feel? If God's holy wrath against you has been satisfied, and you live in the freedom of knowing His graceful love more than His wrath, how are you at forgiving those who have angered you? If you are holding onto anger toward someone and no restitution has been made, pray that God will enable you to surrender the anger and rest in His love and peace.

63

CHRIST'S FINISHED WORK ON THE CROSS

Word of the Cross #2 RECONCILIATION: "Our relationship with God is restored."

The word reconciliation means to re-establish friendship between two parties, to settle or resolve a dispute, and/or to bring acceptance. Most of us are aware of personal relationships that have required reconciliation. How sad it is when a broken relationship continues to remain broken and isn't reconciled. What joy we experience when we see a broken relationship repaired and healthy again. Reconciliation is certainly a reason for rejoicing!

Read the Truth

For if, while we were God's enemies, we were reconciled to Him through the death of His Son, how much more, having been reconciled, shall we be saved through His life! Not only is this so, but we also boast in God through our Lord Jesus Christ, through whom we have now received reconciliation. (Romans 5:10-11)

All this is from God, who reconciled us to Himself through Christ and gave us the ministry of reconciliation: that God was reconciling the world to Himself in Christ, not counting people's sins against them. And He has committed to us the message of reconciliation. (2 Corinthians 5:18-19)

For God was pleased to have all His fullness dwell in Him, and through Him to reconcile to Himself all things, whether things on earth or things in heaven, by making peace through His blood, shed on the cross. Once you were alienated from God and were enemies in your minds because of your evil behavior. But now He has reconciled you by Christ's physical body through death to present you holy in His sight, without blemish and free from accusation.(Colossians 1:19-22)

Confirm the Truth

What did our God do for us according to Romans 5:10-11?

What did our God do for us according to 2 Corinthians 5:18-19?

What did our God do for us according to Colossians 1:19-22?

64

Understand the Truth

Before Christ, our problem was a state of alienation (separation) from God because of sin (Isaiah 59:2). But God did something about that—He reconciled us to Himself through Jesus' death, and we are saved through His life. We have received reconciliation. Reconciliation is a present reality for Christians and is worthy of our rejoicing. And there is even rejoicing in heaven as we experience repentance (Luke 15:7, 10) that results in reconciliation with our God.

Jesus Christ has fully paid our debt of sin, removing the barrier between God and people. God's "books" have been balanced; the debt has been paid. God stands eagerly welcoming anyone who will believe the good news and come home (repent).

You can dwell on the FACT that the barrier of sin has been taken away and a bridge has been built between you and God because of Jesus' finished work on the cross. This was God's act of reconciliation offered to you.

And even more than that, God was pleased to reconcile all things on earth and heaven through Jesus' blood so He can present us holy and blameless in His sight.

Reflect and Respond

CHRIST'S FINISHED WORK ON THE CROSS

>⊗→→⊗→→⊗→⊱⊱⊗⊰⊰⊗⊰

Word of the Cross #2 RECONCILIATION: "Our relationship with God is restored."

Read the Truth

But God demonstrates His own love for us in this: While we were still sinners, Christ died for us. (Romans 5:8)

All this is from God, who reconciled us to Himself through Christ and gave us the ministry of reconciliation: that God was reconciling the world to Himself in Christ, not counting people's sins against them. And He has committed to us the message of reconciliation. We are therefore Christ's ambassadors, as though God were making His appeal through us. We implore you on Christ's behalf: Be reconciled to God. (2 Corinthians 5:18-20)

Confirm the Truth

According to Romans 5:8, what was God's motivation for reconciliation?

According to 2 Corinthians 5:18-20, God gave us the ministry of reconciliation because He is doing what?

Understand the Truth

God demonstrated His love for us when Christ died for us so that we could be reconciled to Him. This reconciliation extends to the whole world, that is, to everyone who chooses to receive it by faith. According to 2 Corinthians 5:18-20, we have been given the ministry of reconciliation, announcing to our world that God is no longer counting men's sins against them through Christ. We are to appeal to the world in hopes of persuading those who listen to be reconciled to God through faith in Christ.

"Reconcile to Himself all things" does not mean that Christ by His death has saved all people...When Adam and Eve sinned, not only was the harmony between God and man destroyed, but also disorder came into creation (Romans 8:19-22). So when Christ died on the cross, He made peace possible between God and mankind, and He restored in principle the harmony in the physical world, though the full realization of the latter will come only when Christ returns." (*NIV Study Bible*, note on Colossians 1:20, p. 1814)

Reflect and Respond

The same power of reconciliation is available to you through Christ for your relationships. If you are in the midst of a relationship that is broken and in need of reconciliation, pray that God would work His mighty hand in the relationship and provide you with His wisdom in pursuing reconciliation.

What steps can you take to reconcile the relationship?

CHRIST'S FINISHED WORK ON THE CROSS

❦❦❦❦❦❦❦❦❦❦❦❦❦❦❦

Word of the Cross #3 REDEMPTION: "We have been purchased out of slavery to sin and released into freedom."

Redemption can refer to recovering ownership by paying a stipulated sum as in the pawning of an item of value then going back later to pay what is owed on the "loan" to get that item back. Or redemption can mean to set something or someone free from bondage by paying a ransom, such as for a kidnapped person or releasing a slave to become free. That is the focus of biblical redemption.

Read the Truth

For even the Son of Man did not come to be served, but to serve, and to give His life as a ransom for many. (Mark 10:45)

In Him we have redemption through His blood, the forgiveness of sins, in accordance with the riches of God's grace that He lavished on us. (Ephesians 1:7-8)

For you know that it was not with perishable things such as silver or gold that you were redeemed from the empty way of life handed down to you from your ancestors, but with the precious blood of Christ, a lamb without blemish or defect. (1 Peter 1:18-19)

Confirm the Truth

What did Jesus declare about His purpose in Mark 10:45?

How are we redeemed according to Ephesians 1:7?

From what are we redeemed (1 Peter 1:18-19)?

Understand the Truth

Biblical redemption is based on an understanding of the pain of slavery—a common practice in the Roman Empire at the time. Nearly 50% of the people were slaves—1 out of every 2 men, women, and children! The readers of the New Testament were very familiar with the hopelessness of being owned by a slave master, the buying and selling associated with the slave market, and the only two ways out of the miserable cycle—death or being bought by someone who would set you free.

Jesus Christ declared that He came not to be served, but to serve and to give His life as a ransom for many. It is through Christ's blood (the purchase price) that we are redeemed. We are redeemed from the slavery of sin and from the empty way of life handed down to us by our forefathers.

Redemption represents an important change in our relationship with God. Before Christ, humanity was in a state of slavery to sin and to death (spiritual and physical). Biblical redemption means that people have been purchased out of slavery at a price, the blood of Christ, and released into freedom to serve God in obedience.

Reflect and Respond

CHRIST'S FINISHED WORK ON THE CROSS

Word of the Cross #3 REDEMPTION: "We have been purchased out of slavery to sin and released into freedom."

Read the Truth

Christ redeemed us from the curse of the law by becoming a curse for us, for it is written: "Cursed is everyone who is hung on a pole." He redeemed us in order that the blessing given to Abraham might come to the Gentiles through Christ Jesus, so that by faith we might receive the promise of the Spirit. (Galatians 3:13-14)

...while we wait for the blessed hope—the appearing of the glory of our great God and Savior, Jesus Christ, who gave HImself for us to redeem us from all wickedness and to purify for Himself a people that are His very own, eager to do what is good. (Titus 2:13-14)

Confirm the Truth

Based upon Galatians 3:13-14, from what did Jesus Christ redeem us and why?

According to Titus 2:14, from what did Jesus Christ redeem us and why?

Understand the Truth

Jesus Christ redeemed us from the curse of the Law so that by faith we might receive the promise of the Spirit and the blessing given to Abraham of righteousness by faith alone. Jesus Christ also redeemed us from all wickedness to purify for Himself a people that are His very own, eager to do what is good.

In the Bible, to redeem means to free someone from something bad by paying a penalty or a ransom (see Exodus 21:30; 13:13). Likewise, in the Greek world slaves could be redeemed by the payment of a price, either by someone else or by the slave himself. Similarly, Jesus redeems believers from the "curse of the law" (Galatians 3:13) and "all wickedness" (Titus 2:14). The ransom price is not silver or gold, but Christ's blood (Ephesians 1:7; 1 Peter 1:19; Revelation 5:9). (*NIV Study Bible,* note on 1 Peter 1:19, p. 1889)

Reflect and Respond

CHRIST'S FINISHED WORK ON THE CROSS

Word of the Cross #3 REDEMPTION: " We have been purchased out of slavery to sin and released into freedom."

Read the Truth

For He has rescued us from the dominion of darkness and brought us into the kingdom of the Son He loves, in whom we have redemption, the forgiveness of sins. (Colossians 1:13-14)

And they sang a new song, saying: "You are worthy to take the scroll and to open its seals, because you were slain, and with your blood you purchased for God persons from every tribe and language and people and nation. You have made them to be a kingdom and priests to serve our God, and they will reign on the earth." (Revelation 5:9-10)

Confirm the Truth

From what have we been rescued (Colossians 1:13-14)?

To what have we been brought?

According to Revelation 5:9-10, who has Jesus purchased with His blood and for what purpose?

Understand the Truth

As God redeems us, He rescues us from the dominion of darkness and brings us into the kingdom of the Son He loves. We have forgiveness of sins because we are redeemed. God chose to purchase men and women for God from every tribe, language, people, and nation to be a kingdom and priests to serve Him.

Anyone who puts her faith in Jesus Christ will be redeemed. When Jesus Christ died, He purchased redemption for everyone who would put her trust in Him. These are the redeemed ones representing every tribe and language and people and nation in Revelation 5:9-10.

Reflect and Respond

CHRIST'S FINISHED WORK ON THE CROSS

Word of the Cross #3 REDEMPTION: "We have been purchased out of slavery to sin and released into freedom."

Read the Truth

What then? Shall we sin because we are not under the law but under grace? By no means! Don't you know that when you offer yourselves to someone as obedient slaves, you are slaves of the one you obey—whether you are slaves to sin, which leads to death, or to obedience, which leads to righteousness? But thanks be to God that, though you used to be slaves to sin, you have come to obey from your heart the pattern of teaching that has now claimed your allegiance. You have been set free from sin and have become slaves to righteousness. (Romans 6:15-18)

I am using an example from everyday life because of your human limitations. Just as you used to offer yourselves as slaves to impurity and to ever-increasing wickedness, so now offer yourselves as slaves to righteousness leading to holiness. When you were slaves to sin, you were free from the control of righteousness. What benefit did you reap at that time from the things you are now ashamed of? Those things result in death! But now that you have been set free from sin and have become slaves of God, the benefit you reap leads to holiness, and the result is eternal life. For the wages of sin is death, but the gift of God is eternal life in Christ Jesus our Lord. (Romans 6:19-23)

Confirm the Truth

From Romans 6:15-18, being a slave to sin leads to what?

Being a slave of God (obedience) leads to what (Romans 6:15-18)?

From Romans 6:19-23, being a slave to sin leads to what?

Being a slave of God leads to what (Romans 6:19-23)?

Understand the Truth

The life of slavery to sin leads to someone offering their bodies to impurity and ever-increasing wickedness, free from the control of righteousness with no benefits, only shame. The end result is death. The life of freedom leads to someone offering their bodies to God and His righteousness leading to holiness, lavished grace and eternal life. Their life is characterized by hearts willingly obedient to God.

Since Jesus Christ has paid a full ransom price, the believer is a possession of God and is secure in freedom until His complete redemption (of the body) is accomplished. Dwell on the FACT that you, as a believer, have been purchased by the blood of Christ out of slavery to sin and released into freedom as God's act of redemption. The third verse of *In Christ Alone*, illustrates redemption this way:

> There in the ground His body lay; light of the world by darkness slain.
> Then bursting forth in glorious Day; up from the grave He rose again!
> And as He stands in victory sin's curse has lost its grip on me.
> For I am His and He is mine - bought with the precious blood of Christ. (Stuart Townend)

You have a new master now with greater power living inside of you—the Spirit of God Himself—who can give you freedom from any entrapping sin. Claim that freedom now. Choose to obey the Spirit inside you who will lead you and empower you to say "no" to sin.

Reflect and Respond

Are you experiencing the freedom from slavery to sin in your life right now? If not, do you have confidence that you do not have to listen to the voice of your old slave master sin?

CHRIST'S FINISHED WORK ON THE CROSS

Word of the Cross #4 FORGIVENESS: "Human guilt has been transferred to a substitute and taken away."

Forgiveness represents an important change in our relationship with God. Our problem before Christ: All humanity is guilty before a holy God. God's answer is to take away the guilt.

Read the Truth

In fact, the law requires that nearly everything be cleansed with blood, and without the shedding of blood there is no forgiveness. (Hebrews 9:22)

He is to cast lots for the two goats—one lot for the Lord and the other for the scapegoat. Aaron shall bring the goat whose lot falls to the Lord and sacrifice it for a sin offering. But the goat chosen by lot as the scapegoat shall be presented alive before the Lord to be used for making atonement by sending it into the wilderness as a scapegoat. (Leviticus 16:8-10)

When Aaron has finished making atonement for the Most Holy Place, the tent of meeting and the altar, he shall bring forward the live goat. He is to lay both hands on the head of the live goat and confess over it all the wickedness and rebellion of the Israelites—all their sins—and put them on the goat's head. He shall send the goat away into the wilderness in the care of someone appointed for the task. The goat will carry on itself all their sins to a remote place; and the man shall release it in the wilderness. (Leviticus 16:20-22)

The next day John saw Jesus coming toward him and said, "Look, the Lamb of God, who takes away the sin of the world!" (John 1:29)

"No longer will they teach their neighbor, or say to one another, 'Know the Lord,' because they will all know me, from the least of them to the greatest," declares the Lord. "For I will forgive their wickedness and will remember their sins no more." (Jeremiah 31:34)

Confirm the Truth

According to Hebrews 9:22, what was required for God to offer forgiveness?

According to Leviticus 16:8-10, what happened to the goat "for the Lord?"

According to Leviticus 16:20-22, what was the role of the scapegoat?

In John 1:29, what did John the Baptist publicly declare about Jesus?

73

What did God promise in Jeremiah 31:34 about human sins?

Understand the Truth

According to God's own plan, the shedding of blood was required for God to offer forgiveness to anyone. The Greek word translated "forgiveness" means literally, "to send off or send away." The result is "to separate the sin from the sinner" as described in Leviticus 16:20-22 (the role of the "scapegoat"). The scapegoat represented the sins of the people (both intentional and unintentional) being taken away from God's presence in the community. John the Baptist announced as Jesus came to be baptized that Jesus was the lamb of God who takes away the sin of the world through shedding His own blood.

God promised in Jeremiah 31:34 that one day He would forgive our wickedness and remember our sins no more. They will be removed from His mind. That happened when Jesus shed His own blood on the cross so that anyone who trusts in Jesus as Savior would have their sins removed. Isn't that wonderful?

Reflect and Respond

CHRIST'S FINISHED WORK ON THE CROSS

Word of the Cross #4 FORGIVENESS: "Human guilt has been transferred to a substitute and taken away."

Read the Truth

When you were dead in your sins and in the uncircumcision of your flesh, God made you alive with Christ. He forgave us all our sins, having canceled the charge of our legal indebtedness, which stood against us and condemned us; He has taken it away, nailing it to the cross. (Colossians 2:13-14)

...that God was reconciling the world to Himself in Christ, not counting people's sins against them. And He has committed to us the message of reconciliation. (2 Corinthians 5:19)

God made Him who had no sin to be sin for us, so that in Him we might become the righteousness of God. (2 Corinthians 5:21)

Confirm the Truth

According to Colossians 2:13-14, what did God do to our sins for us?

How many of our sins are covered by this action?

What do you learn from 2 Corinthians 5:19 about our sins?

The action of God described in 2 Corinthians 5:21 is called the "Great Exchange." What is being exchanged?

Understand the Truth

On the cross, God canceled the measuring stick that made us continually guilty before God—the Law. That was taken away. As a result, God forgave us all our sins in Christ Jesus. ALL of your sins.

Since the believer's sins have been taken away, God does not hold them (sins) against him/her. Sins are applied to Jesus who takes them on our behalf. Forgiveness is complete and continual. As 2 Corinthians 5:19 says, [God] is "not counting people's sins against them." Only one sin separates any man or woman from eternal life with God—rejecting faith in Jesus Christ (John 3:16-18). What a relief that is!

Instead, God places all of our sins on His Son Jesus. God places Jesus' righteousness on us in the place of our sins. That is the Great Exchange. What a marvelous act of grace on God's part. We do not deserve this. It is a gift of love. The only requirement to receive this gift of love is faith—faith in Jesus Christ as Savior.

Reflect and Respond

CHRIST'S FINISHED WORK ON THE CROSS

Word of the Cross #4 FORGIVENESS: "Human guilt has been transferred to a substitute and taken away."

Read the Truth

Repent, then, and turn to God, so that your sins may be wiped out, that times of refreshing may come from the Lord, (Acts 3:19)

"Therefore, my friends, I want you to know that through Jesus the forgiveness of sins is proclaimed to you. Through Him everyone who believes is set free from every sin, a justification you were not able to obtain under the law of Moses. (Acts 13:38-39)

Therefore, brothers and sisters, since we have confidence to enter the Most Holy Place by the blood of Jesus, by a new and living way opened for us through the curtain, that is, His body, and since we have a great priest over the house of God, let us draw near to God with a sincere heart and with the full assurance that faith brings, having our hearts sprinkled to cleanse us from a guilty conscience and having our bodies washed with pure water. (Hebrews 10:19-22

Confirm the Truth

According to Acts 3:19, what happens when someone repents of their sin (turns away from it) and turns to God?

According to Acts 13:38-39, to whom does God grant forgiveness?

What has God promised to do with your guilt as a result of Christ's offering (Hebrews 10:19-22)?

Understand the Truth

God extends His forgiveness to everyone who believes in Christ, turning away from their sin and toward God. According to Ephesians 1:7, forgiveness is something **we possess as believers** through Jesus' blood shed for us. We receive God's forgiveness for all our sins (past, present, and future) from the moment we place our faith in Jesus Christ. Yet, many believers continue to live in guilt.

Dwell on the FACT that Jesus promises to cleanse your conscience from guilt. Will you take Him at His word? If there is any past sin for which you are still feeling guilty, claim God's complete forgiveness today. You can simply tell God,

"Thank You for forgiving me, thank You for cleansing me...Thank You for being bigger than my sins, and being able to turn things around in ways I cannot imagine. With Jesus' help, I receive the assurance that You have forgiven me. Help my heart catch up with my head on this. Help me to see that You allowed me to go down that dark path into sin because You are able to redeem even the worst things we do." (Sue Bohlin, Probe Ministries, Sept. 2012)

Now, CHOOSE to believe you are forgiven and allow Jesus to cleanse your conscience from any residual guilt. Every time you think about it again, thank God for His amazing gift and experience "times of refreshing" from the Lord (Acts 3:19)!

Reflect and Respond

CHRIST'S FINISHED WORK ON THE CROSS

Word of the Cross #5 JUSTIFICATION: "The believer in Jesus Christ is declared righteous before God."

Justification is a legal term that literally means, "to declare righteous, to declare not guilty." English New Testaments use "justified" and "made righteous" interchangeably, but both mean just about the same thing. Justification represents an important change in our relationship with God. Our problem before Christ was our need for perfect acceptability before a holy God.

Read the Truth

Therefore no one will be declared righteous in God's sight by the works of the law; rather, through the law we become conscious of our sin. (Romans 3:20)

But now apart from the law the righteousness of God has been made known, to which the Law and the Prophets testify. This righteousness is given through faith in Jesus Christ to all who believe. There is no difference between Jew and Gentile, for all have sinned and fall short of the glory of God, and all are justified freely by His grace through the redemption that came by Christ Jesus. God presented Christ as a sacrifice of atonement, through the shedding of His blood—to be received by faith. He did this to demonstrate His righteousness, because in His forbearance He had left the sins committed beforehand unpunished—He did it to demonstrate His righteousness at the present time, so as to be just and the one who justifies those who have faith in Jesus. (Romans 3:21-26)

Confirm the Truth

What is declared in Romans 3:20 about being righteous in God's sight?

How does anyone receive righteousness (or be justified) according to Romans 3:21-26?

God's justice demands punishment for sin. Based on what you have learned, how is His justice satisfied?

Who gets to receive the "not guilty" verdict?

Understand the Truth

God's forgiveness and justification of the believer are not due to compromise on God's part or a relaxing of His holy standards. These are possible because the sacrifice of Jesus Christ fully honored and *satisfied the righteous demands of a holy God.*

In our culture, we use the term "acquitted" for someone who is declared not guilty. And this acquittal is for the one wrong act of which the person is being accused. Yet, we do many other wrong things. For us as believers, God declares us "not guilty" of all sin, once and for all, based on our faith alone in His Son! What a deal!

> "The term 'justified' describes what happens when someone believes in Christ as His Savior: from the negative viewpoint, He [God] declares the person to be not guilty; from the positive viewpoint, He [God] declares him to be righteous. He cancels the guilt of the person's sin and credits righteousness to him...God will declare everyone who puts his trust in Jesus not guilty but righteous...Christ's righteousness (His obedience to God's law and His sacrificial death) will be credited to believers as their own. Paul uses the word 'credited' nine times in [Romans] chapter 4 alone." (*NIV Study Bible,* Romans 3:24 note, p. 1710)

So God not only declares us "not guilty" of all sin through our faith in His Son, He also gives us a new status called "righteousness before God." It is not our own righteousness that does it. When God looks on you and me, He sees His Son's righteousness taking the place of our sin—even our sin after we've been believers for a long time.

Picture an accountant's spreadsheet dedicated to your life. On the left side of the page is the heading "your sins;" on the right side of the page is the heading "Christ's righteousness." When you and I sin (intentionally or unintentionally) for the rest of our lives, God replaces that sin on the "your sins" side with Christ's righteousness and puts your sin on His side—your sin is taken away (forgiveness). It is a continual balancing. Your sin never stays on your side of the page because God declares in 2 Corinthians 5:19 that He is "not counting men's sins against them." You are forever declared "not guilty" in His sight. Isn't that great news?!

Reflect and Respond

CHRIST'S FINISHED WORK ON THE CROSS

❧☙❧☙❧☙❧☙❧☙❧☙❧

Word of the Cross #5 JUSTIFICATION: "The believer in Jesus Christ is declared righteous before God."

Read the Truth

Therefore, since we have been justified through faith, we have peace with God through our Lord Jesus Christ, through whom we have gained access by faith into this grace in which we now stand. And we boast in the hope of the glory of God. (Romans 5:1-2)

For God was pleased to have all His fullness dwell in Him, and through Him to reconcile to Himself all things, whether things on earth or things in heaven, by making peace through His blood, shed on the cross. Once you were alienated from God and were enemies in your minds because of your evil behavior. But now He has reconciled you by Christ's physical body through death to present you holy in His sight, without blemish and free from accusation... (Colossians 1:19-22)

Confirm the Truth

According to Romans 5:1-2, what do we get as a result of being justified?

What does Paul declare about our change of relationship with God (Colossians 1:20-22)?

Understand the Truth

According to Romans 5:1-2, we now have peace with God as a benefit of being justified. We are no longer enemies but are reconciled to Him as saved ones. We are no longer alienated from God as enemies in our minds because of our evil behavior. Instead, we are now presented as "holy in His sight," without blemish and free from accusation.

Justification is God's act as Judge, where He declares a guilty sinner to be totally righteous in His sight, on the basis of Christ's finished work on the cross and that person's faith in Him. Justification is by faith alone and not depending upon any works a believer can do to earn acceptability in God's sight, even after they are saved.

Reflect and Respond

CHRIST'S FINISHED WORK ON THE CROSS

Word of the Cross #5 JUSTIFICATION: "The believer in Jesus Christ is declared righteous before God."

Read the Truth

Watch out for those dogs, those evildoers, those mutilators of the flesh. For it is we who are the circumcision, we who serve God by His Spirit, who boast in Christ Jesus, and who put no confidence in the flesh—though I myself have reasons for such confidence. If someone else thinks they have reasons to put confidence in the flesh, I have more: circumcised on the eighth day, of the people of Israel, of the tribe of Benjamin, a Hebrew of Hebrews; in regard to the law, a Pharisee; as for zeal, persecuting the church; as for righteousness based on the law, faultless. (Philippians 3:2-6)

But whatever were gains to me I now consider loss for the sake of Christ. What is more, I consider everything a loss because of the surpassing worth of knowing Christ Jesus my Lord, for whose sake I have lost all things. I consider them garbage, that I may gain Christ and be found in Him, not having a righteousness of my own that comes from the law, but that which is through faith in Christ—the righteousness that comes from God on the basis of faith. (Philippians 3:7-9)

So in Christ Jesus you are all children of God through faith, for all of you who were baptized into Christ have clothed yourselves with Christ. (Galatians 3:26-27)

Confirm the Truth

In Philippians 3:2-6, Paul described his "confidence in the flesh" (his efforts) to achieve righteousness before God. What did Paul list to prove that he had reasons to put confidence in the flesh?

What did Paul conclude about his efforts in Philippians 3:7-9?

What had Paul done to obtain his new righteous standing before God?

What is declared about believers in Galatians 3:26-27?

Understand the Truth

Paul considered his birth status, education, pursuit of knowledge, and zeal to get rid of Christians as evidence that he had plenty of reasons to convince himself that he was a "righteous" Jew and that God should have been pleased with his efforts. But after knowing Christ, Paul declared all those things that he once thought were in his favor to be rubbish, a loss not a win when it comes to faith. Instead, he discovered that knowing Jesus Christ as Lord was far better. He now preferred to be found in Christ with the righteousness that comes through faith not by his own efforts. All Paul had to do to gain his new righteous standing before God was to trust in Jesus Christ as His Savior and Lord. That is true for you as well.

In Galatians 3, the Bible declares that every believer is a child of God by faith and, therefore, clothed with Christ. When God looks on you and me, He sees Jesus and His righteousness, not all of our faults. It is an amazing plan that is totally based on His grace toward us, not anything we have earned by our own efforts.

Reflect and Respond

If you are still wrestling with the notion that you are not good enough to please God, remember that no one can ever be good enough on his or her own merits to please God. Dwell on the FACT of your justification—being declared righteous so that you are now perfectly acceptable to a holy God based on your faith in His Son.

How do you feel about this? When you are tempted to think that God could not possibly accept you because of your weaknesses and guilty past, what should you declare to yourself?

CHRIST'S FINISHED WORK ON THE CROSS

Word of the Cross #6 SANCTIFICATION: "Set apart as God's possession for His exclusive use."

Like propitiation, sanctification is a word we do not use in our daily vocabulary. To be sanctified means to be made holy. To be "holy" means to be "set apart for special use." Because the two words—*sanctified* and *holy*—are so closely connected, they are used interchangeably in our English translations. They mean the same thing, though.

Read the Truth

I will rescue you from your own people and from the Gentiles. I am sending you to them to open their eyes and turn them from darkness to light, and from the power of Satan to God, so that they may receive forgiveness of sins and a place among those who are sanctified by faith in me. (Acts 26:17-18)

And by that will, we have been made holy through the sacrifice of the body of Jesus Christ once for all. (Hebrews 10:10)

...for it is written: "Be holy, because I am holy." (1 Peter 1:16)

Confirm the Truth

According to Acts 26:17-18, believers in Jesus Christ have their eyes opened to turn from what and to what?

As stated in Hebrews 10:10, how are we made holy/sanctified in God's sight?

What does God desire of us (1 Peter 1:16)?

Understand the Truth

Sanctification represents another important change in our standing with God. Our problem before Christ was our need to be separated **from** the world and separated **to** God. This is accomplished through Christ's sacrifice as all believers are turned **from** darkness **to** light and **from** the power of Satan **to** God. God demands that we be holy as He is holy (1 Peter 1:16). God makes us holy in His sight by our faith in Jesus Christ.

But sanctification is more than just having a different status before God. It provides a different purpose as well. Every believer has been set apart as

God's special, beloved possession for His exclusive use. To be set apart for special use is similar to using fine china and silverware for special occasions. It is the opposite of ordinary and common. You are God's special, beloved possession—called by Him to be dedicated to His service. How sweet is that!

Reflect and Respond

CHRIST'S FINISHED WORK ON THE CROSS

✺❀➤✺❀➤➤❀✺❀✺❀✺❀✺❀✺❀

Word of the Cross #6 SANCTIFICATION: "Set apart as God's possession for His exclusive use."

Read the Truth

To all in Rome who are loved by God and called to be His holy people: Grace and peace to you from God our Father and from the Lord Jesus Christ. (Romans 1:7)

Paul, an apostle of Christ Jesus by the will of God, and Timothy our brother, To the church of God in Corinth, together with all His holy people throughout Achaia (2 Corinthians 1:1)

Paul, an apostle of Christ Jesus by the will of God, To God's holy people in Ephesus, the faithful in Christ Jesus: (Ephesians 1:1)

And we, who with unveiled faces all reflect the Lord's glory, are being transformed into His likeness with ever increasing glory, which comes from the Lord, who is the Spirit. (2 Corinthians 3:18)

For those God foreknew He also predestined to be conformed to the likeness of His Son, that He might be the firstborn among many brothers. (Romans 8:29)

Confirm the Truth

Who, in particular, are being called "holy people" (same as the word "saints") in Romans 1:7; 2 Corinthians 1:1; and Ephesians 1:1?

Believers are also "being made holy" by the Holy Spirit as an ongoing reality. Into what is the Holy Spirit transforming us according to 2 Corinthians 3:18?

In "being made holy" by the Holy Spirit, to what are we being conformed in Romans 8:29?

Understand the Truth

Sanctified ones are called "holy people" and "saints" in the New Testament, depending on the translation. Whenever you see "saints," "holy ones" or "holy people," those words are translating the Greek word *hagios*. Paul used the word *hagios* to describe the believers in Rome, Corinth, and Ephesus. Many translators choose to use the English word "saint" to represent Paul's intended meaning.

> The word "saint" comes from the Greek word *hagios*, "holy," meaning separated from sin and dedicated to God. All believers are called "holy ones" (*hagioi*) based upon their faith in Jesus Christ, not on any exceptional behavior. A saint is identified by position, what God declares to be true about you. Every believer is one of God's saints, totally loved and accepted by him—considered a saint of God by position, not by behavior. (*Vines Expository Dictionary of Old and New Testament Words,* pp. 307-308)

Believers are made holy by Christ's death on the cross. That means you are one of God's saints by faith in Jesus Christ. That is your status before God.

Believers are also "being made holy" in their thoughts, words, and actions by the work of the Holy Spirit. This is ongoing from the moment of salvation until the Lord comes or until we die when our "being made holy" is complete. The goal of the Spirit's work is to transform us into the likeness of Christ so that we become in thought and behavior what we are in status—holy as God is holy.

Dwell on the FACT that God declares you holy because of your faith in Christ. You are set apart by Him, for Him. This is your status before God because of your faith. Your behavior matches your position when you submit to the Spirit's work to intentionally separate you from what God calls sin and then commit yourself to being used for His purposes—24/7.

Reflect and Respond

Reflect on how you can commit yourself to God's use throughout a typical day as you care for your household, be a parent or grandparent to children, work for an employer, interact with people around you, spend your leisure time...

DAY 58

CHRIST'S FINISHED WORK ON THE CROSS

Read the Truth

He himself bore our sin in His body on the cross, so that we might die to sins and live for righteousness; by His wounds you have been healed. (1 Peter 2:24)

Confirm the Truth

Because of what Jesus did on the cross, what is true about you?

Understand the Truth

Because of the cross, you can dwell on the FACT that God was fully **satisfied** by Jesus' finished work on the cross. God is no longer angry at your sin because you believe in His Son. You can dwell on the FACT that the barrier of sin has been taken away and complete **reconciliation** between you and God is possible because of Jesus' finished work on the cross. Your relationship with God is restored. You can dwell on the FACT that you, as a believer, have been purchased by the blood of Christ out of slavery to sin and released into freedom as God's act of **redemption**. You have a new master with greater power living inside of you, the Spirit of God Himself, who can give you freedom from any entrapping sin.

You can also dwell on the FACT that you are completely **forgiven** of your sins and that Jesus promises to cleanse your conscience from guilt. You can dwell on the FACT that you have been declared righteous (**justified**) and are now perfectly acceptable to a holy God based on your faith in His Son. And you can dwell on the FACT that God declares you holy because of your faith in Christ. You are **sanctified**—set apart by Him, for Him.

Human disease was sin. Because of this disease, we were: 1) never able to make ourselves well, 2) in bondage to the disease, 3) alienated from the one who could heal us, 4) carrying the guilt of having the disease, 5) experiencing cumulative effects of the disease, and 6) unable to live a purposeful life. Jesus' finished work on the cross removed all these effects of the disease so that "by His wounds you have been healed" (1 Peter 2:24)—truly healed!

An understanding of Christ's finished work on the cross is the basis for a firm knowledge of our identity in Him—a foundational truth for successful Christian living. It was totally **God's work** to make sinners acceptable again in His sight. Our proper response is to **trust** and **rest in His work**, and to continually offer Him thanks from grateful hearts along with our willing service. We can appreciate the power and importance of the six words of the cross. And we can consider that they all have been accomplished to make the seventh great word possible: *"Regeneration,"* the restoration of spiritual *life*. This is the subject of the next section.

Reflect and Respond

part 5

GRACE-GIVEN LIFE TO YOU

*But because of His great love for us, God,
who is rich in mercy, made us alive with Christ
even when we were dead in transgressions —
it is by grace you have been saved. And God
raised us up with Christ and seated us with
Him in the heavenly realms in Christ Jesus.
(Ephesians 2:4-6)*

GRACE-GIVEN LIFE TO YOU

From the time sin entered into the relationship of humanity with our Creator God, men and women have had a spiritual problem that can be compared to death caused by a fatal disease: (1) Sin ("the disease" Romans 3:23) and (2) Death ("result of the disease" Romans 6:23). Our twofold problem demanded a twofold solution:

1) For our sin disease, people need forgiveness and righteousness. *Answer: Christ's* **death** *(the cross).* We can now be cured of the disease.

2) For our state of death, people need regeneration (the restoration of **life**). *Answer: Christ's* **resurrection**. We can now be given life that is forever.

The Gospel message included the answer to both spiritual problems.

Jesus Christ **laid down** His life **for** you...so that He could **give** His life **to** you...so that He could **live** His life **through** you. (Ian Thomas, *The Saving Life of Christ)*)

Read the Truth

But because of His great love for us, God, who is rich in mercy, made us alive with Christ even when we were dead in transgressions — it is by grace you have been saved. And God raised us up with Christ and seated us with Him in the heavenly realms in Christ Jesus. (Ephesians 2:4-6)

Confirm the Truth

Because of His great love for you, God has done what (Ephesians 2:4-6)?

Understand the Truth

Many Christians have a lack of understanding of two **vital** truths: (1) Christ's finished work on the cross to secure our complete acceptance before God, and (2) "Christ in you" as the dynamic of daily Christian living. As a result, believers may have a fairly solid understanding of God's grace as it relates to their initial salvation experience but an inconsistent, wavering understanding of God's grace in their ongoing life as a Christian. Many Christians also have very little understanding of the significance of having received the very life of God through the Holy Spirit. As a result of such misunderstanding, Christians are often overwhelmed by failure, discouragement, and despair resulting from attempts to be perfected "by human effort."

The great difference between present-day Christianity and that of which we read in these [New Testament letters] is that to us it is primarily a performance; to them it was a real experience. We are apt to reduce the Christian religion to a code or, at best, a rule of heart and life. To these [new Christians], it is quite plainly the invasion of their lives by a new quality of life altogether. They do not hesitate to describe this as Christ living in them. (J.B. Phillips, Introduction to *Letters to Young Churches*)

Remember that you have complete acceptance before God because of Christ's finished work on the cross. Now we will focus on the life given to us by Christ Himself as our **power for daily Christian living**.

Reflect and Respond

Natural Man or Woman (in Adam)

Read the Truth

So God created mankind in His own image, in the image of God He created them; male and female He created them. (Genesis 1:27)

And the Lord God commanded the man, "You are free to eat from any tree in the garden; but you must not eat from the tree of the knowledge of good and evil, for when you eat from it you will certainly die." (Genesis 2:16-17)

Now the serpent was more crafty than any of the wild animals the Lord God had made. He said to the woman, "Did God really say, 'You must not eat from any tree in the garden'?" The woman said to the serpent, "We may eat fruit from the trees in the garden, but God did say, 'You must not eat fruit from the tree that is in the middle of the garden, and you must not touch it, or you will die.'" "You will not certainly die," the serpent said to the woman. "For God knows that when you eat from it your eyes will be opened, and you will be like God, knowing good and evil." When the woman saw that the fruit of the tree was good for food and pleasing to the eye, and also desirable for gaining wisdom, she took some and ate it. She also gave some to her husband, who was with her, and he ate it. Then the eyes of both of them were opened, and they realized they were naked; so they sewed fig leaves together and made coverings for themselves. (Genesis 3:1-7)

Confirm the Truth

What is said about how God created humans in Genesis 1:27?

What did God give to humans when He created them (Genesis 2:16-17)?

What choice did the first humans, Adam and Eve, make in Genesis 3:1-7?

Understand the Truth

When God created humanity in His own image (Genesis 1:27), we were created with a body, a soul (conscious life made up of mind, emotions and will), and a spirit that enables every man and woman to relate to God. The inner spirit is the source of inner drives for love, acceptance, and identity. It is also the source for meaning and purpose in life. The human spirit was created to be a container for God's Spirit and was the means through which both man and woman enjoyed perfect fellowship with God.

91

Based on that relationship, God had access through Adam's spirit into his soul (teaching his mind, guiding his emotions, directing his will) and, thereby, influencing his body through behavior. The same was true of Eve. So every thought, emotion, word and deed of Adam and Eve *as created* were a perfect representation of the invisible God. They were then truly fulfilling their purpose in life: walking in a **dependent** love relationship with their Creator and, through that relationship, *bearing the image of God.*

Through free choice (Genesis 2:16-17; 3:1-7), Adam and Eve forfeited the life of God and introduced sin and death into the creation. Adam died *physically* 930 years later (Genesis 5:5). However, he and Eve died *spiritually* that day in the garden—they lost the life of God.

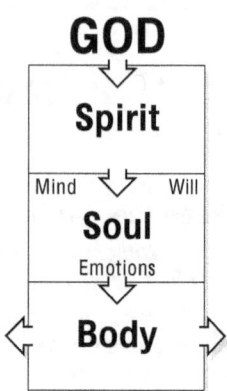

Reflect and Respond

NATURAL MAN OR WOMAN (IN ADAM)

Natural man (in Adam)

Read the Truth

> *Therefore, just as sin entered the world through one man, and death through sin, and in this way death came to all men, because all sinned... (Romans 5:12)*

> *Consequently, just as the result of one trespass was condemnation for all men, so also the result of one act of righteousness was justification that brings life for all men. (Romans 5:18)*

> *As for you, you were dead in your transgressions and sins, in which you used to live when you followed the ways of this world and of the ruler of the kingdom of the air, the spirit who is now at work in those who are disobedient. All of us also lived among them at one time, gratifying the cravings of our sinful nature and following its desires and thoughts. Like the rest, we were by nature objects of wrath. (Ephesians 2:1-3)*

Confirm the Truth

According to Romans 5:12, what are the effects of Adam's sin on all of his descendants, including you?

According to Romans 5:18, what are the effects of Adam's sin (trespass) on all of his descendants, including you?

According to Ephesians 2:1-3, what are the effects of Adam's sin on all of his descendants, including you?

Understand the Truth

You might be wondering why God held Adam responsible for the sinfulness of the whole human race when it was really Eve who sinned first. A possible explanation is this:

> Adam was the person in authority over and therefore responsible for Eve (Gen. 2:18-23; 1 Cor. 11:3). Furthermore, Eve was deceived (2 Cor. 11:3), but Adam sinned deliberately (1 Tim. 2:14). (Tom Constable, *Dr. Constable's Notes on Romans*, p. 59)

The result is that everyone born into this world is considered to be born "in Adam"—i.e., out of his family line. The Bible often refers to this condition as "natural man." Therefore, since that day in the garden, all men and women are born spiritually dead and are sinners by nature.

The "God-shaped vacuum"

> We may not understand how we can inherit evil from our fathers, but there is no argument with the fact that as soon as we are big enough to sin, we go directly into the business of sinning. (A.W. Tozer, 20th century author)

Anyone who has been around small children knows for a fact that this is true!

All men and women are also born spiritually wanting.

> There is a God-shaped vacuum in the heart of every man which cannot be filled by any created thing, but only by God, the Creator, made known through Jesus. (Blaise Pascal, 17th century French physicist)

The diagram at right illustrates this "vacuum." Every human being seeks to fill this vacuum with something that gives them meaning and purpose in life. As Paul wrote in Ephesians 2:1-3, we were "gratifying the cravings of our sinful nature and following its desires and thoughts." Not a pretty picture, is it?

Reflect and Respond

What have you sought to fill this vacuum in your life before you put your faith in Christ?

94

NATURAL MAN OR WOMAN (IN ADAM)

Natural man (in Adam)

Read the Truth

However, as it is written: "No eye has seen, no ear has heard, no mind has conceived what God has prepared for those who love Him" -- but God has revealed it to us by His Spirit. The Spirit searches all things, even the deep things of God. For who among men knows the thoughts of a man except the man's spirit within him? In the same way no one knows the thoughts of God except the Spirit of God. We have not received the spirit of the world but the Spirit who is from God, that we may understand what God has freely given us. This is what we speak, not in words taught us by human wisdom but in words taught by the Spirit, expressing spiritual truths in spiritual words. (1 Corinthians 2:9-13)

The man without the Spirit does not   accept the things that come from the Spirit of God, for they are foolishness to him, and he cannot understand them, because they are spiritually discerned. The spiritual man makes judgments about all things, but he himself is not subject to any man's judgment: "For who has known the mind of the Lord that he may instruct Him?" But we have the mind of Christ. (1 Corinthians 2:14-16)

The god of this age has blinded the minds of unbelievers, so that they cannot see the light of the gospel of the glory of Christ, who is the image of God. (2 Corinthians 4:4)

Confirm the Truth

According to 1 Corinthians 2:9-13, what is true about the person who has the Spirit of God?

According to 1 Corinthians 2:14-16, what is true about the person who does not have the Spirit of God?

What hindrance to her understanding does the unbeliever have?

Understand the Truth

The terms "natural man" or "earthly man" used in the New Testament translations refer to any unsaved man or woman. As Paul described in 1 Corinthians, the natural man or woman doesn't understand or accept the things that come from the Spirit of God. They are like foolishness. The

95

spiritual man or woman is taught by the Spirit who reveals to us God's secret wisdom, the deep things of God, so that we may understand what God has freely given to us. Know God, know life. But no God, no life. So the "natural woman" not only does not have the Spirit of God but also her mind is blinded by Satan so she cannot see the light of the gospel (2 Corinthians 4:4). Satan is the unseen power behind all unbelief and ungodliness.

The unbeliever is already: (1) alienated from God (Colossians 1:20), (2) under the wrath of God (Ephesians 2:3), and (3) spiritually dead to God (Ephesians 2:1). Her problem is not just that she is a sinner in need of forgiveness. **She is dead and in need of life!**

When we become Christians at a young age or forget what it was like to live as an unbeliever before Christ came into our lives, we can be very harsh on those who are living without Christ in this world. We expect nonbelievers to think like we do. Considering how God describes the unbeliever in His Word, their blindness and lack of understanding should generate compassion in us rather than condemnation.

Reflect and Respond

If you became a Christian as an adult, what was life like for you before you experienced Christ's liberation? What drew you to Him? In what ways do you recognize the above elements of the "natural man" in your life at that time?

96

JESUS CHRIST – THE SECOND (LAST) ADAM

Read the Truth

So it is written: "The first man Adam became a living being"; the last Adam, a life-giving spirit. The spiritual did not come first, but the natural, and after that the spiritual. The first man was of the dust of the earth; the second man is of heaven. As was the earthly man, so are those who are of the earth; and as is the heavenly man, so also are those who are of heaven. And just as we have borne the image of the earthly man, so shall we bear the image of the heavenly man. (1 Corinthians 15:45-49)

The Word became flesh and made His dwelling among us. We have seen His glory, the glory of the one and only Son, who came from the Father, full of grace and truth. (John 1:14)

Confirm the Truth

What is true about the first Adam/man (1 Corinthians 15:45-49)?

What is true about the last/second Adam (1 Corinthians 15:45-49)?

What did Jesus (the Word) do to identify with humanity (John 1:14)?

Understand the Truth

Although He was God from all eternity, the Son of God took on a human nature and flesh, totally identifying with us in our humanity. The first Adam received life, was made of the dust of the earth, and all humans born since have been like him (human destined for death). The second Adam (Jesus) gives life, came from heaven to receive an earthly body then received a heavenly body after His death, and we will bear His likeness by faith. Jesus, who was with God and was God (John 1:1-3), became flesh and dwelled among us (John 1:14). In this way, He chose to identify with every human who has ever lived.

Reflect and Respond

JESUS CHRIST – THE SECOND (LAST) ADAM

Read the Truth

In your relationships with one another, have the same mindset as Christ Jesus: Who, being in very nature God, did not consider equality with God something to be used to His own advantage; rather, He made Himself nothing by taking the very nature of a servant, being made in human likeness. And being found in appearance as a man, He humbled Himself by becoming obedient to death— even death on a cross! (Philippians 2:5-8)

Since the children have flesh and blood, He too shared in their humanity so that by His death He might break the power of him who holds the power of death—that is, the devil— and free those who all their lives were held in slavery by their fear of death. For surely it is not angels He helps, but Abraham's descendants. For this reason, He had to be made like them, fully human in every way, in order that He might become a merciful and faithful high priest in service to God, and that He might make atonement for the sins of the people. Because He Himself suffered when He was tempted, He is able to help those who are being tempted. (Hebrews 2:14-18)

Confirm the Truth

Based on Philippians 2:5-8, what did Jesus do to identify with humanity?

Why did Jesus need to be made like us (Hebrews 2:14-18)?

Understand the Truth

In Philippians 2:5-8, we are told that Jesus, the Son of God, voluntarily took on human likeness. He did this so He could identify with us, being fully human in every way (Hebrews 2:14-18). Through His virgin birth, Jesus Christ entered the world spiritually alive and without sin (John 8:46; Hebrews 4:15; 2 Corinthians 5:21). He was the first complete man, from God's point of view, to live on earth since the Fall of Adam and Eve. Thus, He is called the "Second Adam."

Reflect and Respond

Jesus Christ – the Second Adam.

Read the Truth

The man went away and told the Jewish leaders that it was Jesus who had made him well. So because Jesus was doing these things on the Sabbath, the Jewish leaders began to persecute Him. In His defense Jesus said to them, "My Father is always at His work to this very day, and I too am working." For this reason they tried all the more to kill Him; not only was He breaking the Sabbath, but He was even calling God His own Father, making Himself equal with God. Jesus gave them this answer: "Very truly I tell you, the Son can do nothing by Himself; He can do only what He sees His Father doing, because whatever the Father does the Son also does. (John 5:15-19)

By myself I can do nothing; I judge only as I hear, and my judgment is just, for I seek not to please myself but Him who sent me. (John 5:30)

Confirm the Truth

What did Jesus declare in John 5:15-19 about the work that He does?

What does Jesus declare in John 5:30 about what He seeks to do?

Understand the Truth

In His humanity, Jesus demonstrated for us the way we should live in dependence on God. Jesus said in John 5 that He was doing the work of God (showing compassion and teaching truth). And Jesus was seeking to please God rather than Himself with His life. He demonstrated to anyone watching or listening what it was like to live the kind of life that God designed us to do.

If Jesus lived as a man dependent on God, how much more should we recognize our need to do the same? Consider the areas of your life where you tend to live in self-sufficiency. Generally, it is in your areas of strength—your skills and abilities. The danger we face is getting too confident in our own abilities so that we don't rely on God in that area.

Reflect and Respond

Consider one area of your life in which you act through your own strengths and abilities without relying on the power of God to work through those same strengths and abilities. What choices do you need to make to rely on God more in that area of your life?

JESUS CHRIST – THE SECOND ADAM.

Read the Truth

Then Jesus cried out, "Whoever believes in me does not believe in me only, but in the one who sent me. The one who looks at me is seeing the one who sent me. I have come into the world as a light, so that no one who believes in me should stay in darkness. (John 12:44-46)

For I did not speak on my own, but the Father who sent me commanded me to say all that I have spoken. I know that His command leads to eternal life. So whatever I say is just what the Father has told me to say." (John 12:49-50)

Philip said, "Lord, show us the Father and that will be enough for us." Jesus answered: "Don't you know me, Philip, even after I have been among you such a long time? Anyone who has seen me has seen the Father. How can you say, 'Show us the Father'? Don't you believe that I am in the Father, and that the Father is in me? The words I say to you I do not speak on my own authority. Rather, it is the Father, living in me, who is doing His work. Believe me when I say that I am in the Father and the Father is in me; or at least believe on the evidence of the works themselves. (John 14:8-11)

Confirm the Truth

Who does Jesus reflect in His life (John 12:44-46)?

In John 12:49-50, whom do His words reflect?

In John 14:8-11, whom do His words and works reflect?

Understand the Truth

In John 12, Jesus declares Himself to be the visible representation of the invisible God, showing us the true way to God. In His humanity, Jesus speaks God's words to others and yields to God's will in His words. We can also speak God's words to others and yield our wills to whatever God's Word says. Jesus showed us many ways we can live dependently on God and why we should do so. Jesus reflects God living in Him through both His words and His works.

Jesus completely identified with us in our humanity, sin and death, so that we could be totally identified with Him in His resurrected humanity, righteousness **and life** (Isaiah 53:6; Romans 6:4).

God provided a cure for our sin disease through Christ's finished work on the cross, BUT we were still dead and in need of life! God's solution is regeneration. We'll cover that in the next days.

Reflect and Respond

WHAT CHRIST'S RESURRECTION ACCOMPLISHED

To learn more about Christ's resurrection and its meaning for us, please read my blog, "Resurrection, What Does It Mean?" available on my website, melanienewton.com.

Regeneration: The restoration of life is God's solution to humanity's state of spiritual death

The English word "regeneration" [Greek *palingenesia*, from *palin* (again) and *genesis* (birth)] means simply a new birth, a new beginning, or a new order. Regeneration is often used to describe the restoration of a thing to its pristine state, as in the restoration of a piece of furniture or a car. In the New Testament, REGENERATION refers to the giving of **life** after death. Salvation is described as receiving "life."

Read the Truth

Jesus replied, "Very truly I tell you, no one can see the kingdom of God unless they are born again." "How can someone be born when they are old?" Nicodemus asked. "Surely they cannot enter a second time into their mother's womb to be born!" Jesus answered, "Very truly I tell you, no one can enter the kingdom of God unless they are born of water and the Spirit. Flesh gives birth to flesh, but the Spirit gives birth to spirit. (John 3:3-6)

Very truly I tell you, whoever hears my word and believes Him who sent me has eternal life and will not be judged but has crossed over from death to life. (John 5:24)

But because of His great love for us, God, who is rich in mercy, made us alive with Christ even when we were dead in transgressions—it is by grace you have been saved. (Ephesians 2:4-5)

Therefore, if anyone is in Christ, the new creation has come: The old has gone, the new is here! (2 Corinthians 5:17)

Confirm the Truth

How does Jesus describe "receiving life" in John 3:3-6?

What does Jesus say about this in John 5:24?

What is revealed about this in Ephesians 2:4-5?

As a result of being born again, what is now true of you according to 2 Corinthians 5:17?

Understand the Truth

Jesus said that He came to give us life, abundant and full. To Nicodemus (John 3), Jesus said this life-giving experience was being "born again." Everyone is born once in the flesh (physical birth). But salvation requires a new life-giving experience—being born of the Spirit. In John 5, Jesus declared that anyone who believes in Him is given this new life (born again), crossing over completely and permanently from death to life. And Paul says that we are made alive in Christ and are a new creation from that moment onward. Praise God for a new life!

The restoration of life is God's solution to humanity's state of spiritual death. The Spirit of God enters the human spirit and brings eternal life with Him. Because of God's great love for us, He takes humans like you and I who were once spiritually dead and makes us alive in Christ. It is His love that does this. It is His grace that gives this. It is His power that makes this happen. What a gift!

Reflect and Respond

WHAT CHRIST'S RESURRECTION ACCOMPLISHED

Regeneration: The restoration of life is God's solution to humanity's state of spiritual death

Read the Truth

And I will ask the Father, and He will give you another advocate to help you and be with you forever—the Spirit of truth. The world cannot accept Him, because it neither sees Him nor knows Him. But you know Him, for He lives with you and will be in you. (John 14:16-17)

You, however, are not in the realm of the flesh but are in the realm of the Spirit, if indeed the Spirit of God lives in you. And if anyone does not have the Spirit of Christ, they do not belong to Christ. But if Christ is in you, then even though your body is subject to death because of sin, the Spirit gives life because of righteousness. (Romans 8:9-10)

I have been crucified with Christ and I no longer live, but Christ lives in me. The life I now live in the body, I live by faith in the Son of God, who loved me and gave Himself for me. (Galatians 2:20)

To them God has chosen to make known among the Gentiles the glorious riches of this mystery, which is Christ in you, the hope of glory. (Colossians 1:27)

Confirm the truth

In John 14:16-17, how does Jesus give "life" to you?

How do Paul's words in Romans 8:9-10 confirm what Jesus said about how you receive "life?"

What does Galatians 2:20 say about your new life?

According to Colossians 1:27, who lives in you?

Understand the Truth

Jesus promised that God would give the Holy Spirit to us to be with us and in us forever. Forever! It is the Holy Spirit who makes our spirits alive again through His presence.

As the Holy Spirit indwells us, He unites (fuses) us to Christ. We get this from Romans 6:5 which says, "For if we have been **united** with Him in a death like His, we will certainly also be **united** with Him in a resurrection like His."

Resurrection brings life. And this life of Christ is in us. Paul describes this as Christ living in you—"Christ in you." God fills our spirits with Himself (see diagram at right).

> "The Holy Spirit is the bond by which Christ effectually unites us to Himself." (John Calvin, *Calvin: Institutes of the Christian Religion*, 3.1.1)

We, who were once dead, are made alive by the indwelling Holy Spirit who unites us to Christ so that "Christ in you" is a fact of our new existence. It happens at the moment of salvation (Romans 8:9) and lasts forever (John 14:16). We are born again as a new creation (2 Corinthians 5:17). With the restoration of life begins a new adventure.

Reflect and Respond

WHAT CHRIST'S RESURRECTION ACCOMPLISHED

Regeneration: The restoration of life is God's solution to humanity's state of spiritual death

Read the Truth

Abide in me, and I in you. As the branch cannot bear fruit by itself, unless it abides in the vine, neither can you, unless you abide in me. I am the vine; you are the branches. Whoever abides in me and I in him, he it is that bears much fruit, for apart from me you can do nothing. (John 15:4-5, ESV)

I have been crucified with Christ and I no longer live, but Christ lives in me. The life I now live in the body, I live by faith in the Son of God, who loved me and gave Himself for me. (Galatians 2:20)

Confirm the Truth

According to John 15:4-5, how should a new creation in Christ live?

Based on Galatians 2:20, how should a new creation in Christ live?

Understand the Truth

A new creation in Christ lives by abiding in Christ (making our home with Him) and living dependently upon Him to do anything of value. We are to live by faith. Faith is dependency upon and commitment to God. That is what Jesus demonstrated for us in His own life.

Don't you believe that I am in the Father, and that the Father is in me? The words I say to you I do not speak on my own authority. Rather, it is the Father, living in me, who is doing His work. (John 14:10).

Consider how a caterpillar transforms into a butterfly. Something totally changes. The butterfly doesn't look anything like the caterpillar that preceded it. In the same way, the Christian is not just a "forgiven caterpillar." She has been transformed into a "butterfly." You and I must grasp the freedom of God's acceptance through Christ and then learn how to present our humanity to the indwelling Christ and experience true and abundant life. Salvation is not just receiving something we did not have before (i.e., forgiveness of sins). It is **becoming someone we were not** before!

Jesus Christ **laid down** His life **for** you so that He could **give** His life **to** you so that He could **live** His life **through** you.

Reflect and Respond

WHAT CHRIST'S RESURRECTION ACCOMPLISHED

Regeneration: The restoration of life is God's solution to humanity's state of spiritual death

Read the Truth

So you also must consider yourselves dead to sin and alive to God in Christ Jesus. Let not sin therefore reign in your mortal body, to make you obey its passions. Do not present your members to sin as instruments for unrighteousness, but present yourselves to God as those who have been brought from death to life, and your members to God as instruments for righteousness. For sin will have no dominion over you, since you are not under law but under grace. (Romans 6:11-14)

Confirm the Truth

What now should be your relationship to sin and the old life we once lived (Romans 6:11-14)?

What are you to do instead?

Understand the Truth

When it comes to our old way of approaching life (listening to sin barking orders to us), we are to push back, say no, and not even present our bodies to sin to do its work. Instead, we are to present ourselves to God as instruments of righteousness. That means deciding to approach life God's way, listening to the guidance of the Spirit inside of us, and obeying His voice speaking through the Word of God as we read and study it. We can depend on the greater power within us to be our master for obedience to God.

It is important that we understand this. Because God shows His grace to us and forgives us of all sin, that does not give us a "license to sin" because we know we will be forgiven. A proper emphasis on Christ's finished work on the cross does not promote sin for a simple reason—in forgiving us, **God did not leave us as we were.** God transforms our hearts through the regeneration of the Holy Spirit. We who believe have God's law written on our hearts (Hebrews 8:10). All this is possible because of Christ's finished work on the cross and His resurrection on the third day. We'll continue our study of how He "lives His life through you" in the next section.

Reflect and Respond

As a believer, you should know with confidence that God's life is now indwelling you forever. Considering the condition of the "natural man" you learned on earlier days, thank God for His indescribable gift of life to you. What are the benefits of having His life in you?

part 6

GRACE-CREATED IDENTITY

*Therefore, if anyone is in Christ, the new
creation has come: The old has gone, the new
is here! (2 Corinthians 5:17)*

A New Identity that Rocks the World

Read the Truth

Therefore, if anyone is in Christ, the new creation has come: The old has gone, the new is here! (2 Corinthians 5:17)

Confirm the Truth

What is true of anyone who is in Christ?

Understand the Truth

In our world, a person's identity drives everything about life. Identities tell us who we are, where we live, how and where we can travel. Our identity determines what we can buy with our finances and qualifies us for employment. That's why it is so devastating when it's stolen! Knowing our spiritual identity is even more important. From the moment of our salvation, we each receive a new spiritual identity. As Paul wrote about anyone who is in Christ, "she is a new creation."

But don't expect the culture to validate your new identity. From a worldly point of view, you and I are the same as we've always been. All our "baggage" is still seen hanging around our necks. But the FACT is that every Christian is a new creation with a new identity in Christ. This new identity declares how God, who is our true authority, now views us! It is what He has done for us and to us that really counts, not what the culture thinks of us or what we think of ourselves. And there are wonderful perks that go along with this new position in life.

So far, you have learned how your faith in Jesus Christ sets you free from your previous sin-stained existence to enjoy a new life. But your ability to live out this freedom depends upon your understanding of who you now are. How we see ourselves directs how we live our faith walk. We need to grasp the FACT that every believer gets a **new life** with a **radical** new identity—something we never had before, and something no one before Jesus' resurrection ever had!! And this new identity sets us free to live a radically new kind of life—a joyful life.

Reflect and Respond

Think of some ways you try (or have tried in the past) to establish your identity. What happens to us when we try to determine who we are by these things?

A NEW IDENTITY THAT ROCKS THE WORLD

The basis of identity

Read the Truth

For since death came through a man, the resurrection of the dead comes also through a man. For as in Adam all die, so in Christ all will be made alive. (1 Corinthians 15:21-22)

Therefore, just as sin entered the world through one man, and death through sin, and in this way death came to all people, because all sinned. (Romans 5:12)

But the gift is not like the trespass. For if the many died by the trespass of the one man, how much more did God's grace and the gift that came by the grace of the one man, Jesus Christ, overflow to the many! Nor can the gift of God be compared with the result of one man's sin: The judgment followed one sin and brought condemnation, but the gift followed many trespasses and brought justification. For if, by the trespass of the one man, death reigned through that one man, how much more will those who receive God's abundant provision of grace and of the gift of righteousness reign in life through the one man, Jesus Christ! (Romans 5:15-17)

Consequently, just as one trespass resulted in condemnation for all people, so also one righteous act resulted in justification and life for all people. For just as through the disobedience of the one man the many were made sinners, so also through the obedience of the one man the many will be made righteous. (Romans 5:18-19)

The law was brought in so that the trespass might increase. But where sin increased, grace increased all the more, so that, just as sin reigned in death, so also grace might reign through righteousness to bring eternal life through Jesus Christ our Lord. (Romans 5:20-21)

Confirm the Truth

In 1 Corinthians 15:21-22, Paul categorizes people into two groups by whom they are in: "as in Adam all die" and "so in Christ all will be made alive.

According to Romans 5:12, what are the results of being in Adam?

From Romans 5:15-17, what are the results of being in Adam?

From Romans 5:18-19, what are the results of being in Adam?

From Romans 5:15-17, what are the results of being in Christ?

From Romans 5:18-19, what are the results of being in Christ?

What do we receive through Jesus Christ our Lord (Romans 5:20-21)?

Understand the Truth

From God's point of view, there are two kinds of people in the world: (1) those who are **in Adam**, and (2) those who are **in Christ**. Who you are **in** determines your identity and your inheritance.

1) To be **in Adam** means that you have inherited his nature (sinful), the consequences of his actions (condemnation), and his destiny (death).

2) To be **in Christ** means that you have inherited His nature (righteous), the consequences of His actions (justification), and His destiny (eternal life).

Not understanding our identity "in Christ" can enslave us to faulty thinking and behavior. Because of a lack of Bible knowledge, many Christians may only know that their sins are forgiven and that they get to go to heaven when they die. Sometimes, they aren't even sure of those two things.

Because a great "Grace Awakening" has taken place since the 1970s, teaching about our new identity in Christ is everywhere in bookstores and on the radio, TV, and Internet. Yet, most believers still have no idea what their new identity is and all the benefits that come with it. Do you? And if you and I don't know that we are no longer **"in Adam"** but are now **"in Christ"** as new creations, how will we know that we've been set free to live a different kind of life? This section will certainly fill your mind and heart with truth about your grace-created new identity—an identity that will fill your life with freedom and joy!

Reflect and Respond

How you see yourself will influence how you think and live. How do you see yourself? In Christ? Or as just another one of the billions of human beings walking around on our planet? Reflect on how the way you see yourself (past and present) influences your life.

A New Identity that Rocks the World

~~~~~~~~~~~~~~~~~~~

God has changed the believer's identity through the baptism of the Holy Spirit

The word translated *baptized* came from the process for dyeing cloth. It didn't matter if the cloth was sprayed, dipped, or immersed. The significance was taking on the identity of the dye. So in Spirit Baptism, we are "dyed" with Christ. The practical outcome is a total identification (uniting) with Him.

Read the Truth

What shall we say, then? Shall we go on sinning so that grace may increase? By no means! We are those who have died to sin; how can we live in it any longer? Or don't you know that all of us who were baptized into Christ Jesus were baptized into His death? We were therefore buried with Him through baptism into death in order that, just as Christ was raised from the dead through the glory of the Father, we too may live a new life. (Romans 6:1-4)

For if we have been united with Him in a death like His, we will certainly also be united with Him in a resurrection like His. For we know that our old self was crucified with Him so that the body ruled by sin might be done away with, that we should no longer be slaves to sin—because anyone who has died has been set free from sin. (Romans 6:5-7)

Now if we died with Christ, we believe that we will also live with Him. For we know that since Christ was raised from the dead, He cannot die again; death no longer has mastery over Him. The death He died, He died to sin once for all; but the life He lives, He lives to God. In the same way, count yourselves dead to sin but alive to God in Christ Jesus. (Romans 6:8-11)

But because of His great love for us, God, who is rich in mercy, made us alive with Christ even when we were dead in transgressions—it is by grace you have been saved. And God raised us up with Christ and seated us with Him in the heavenly realms in Christ Jesus, (Ephesians 2:4-6)

Confirm the Truth

Although water baptism is a picture of what the Spirit does to us, there's no mention of water in the Romans 6 passage. Spirit baptism is much more significant and has far greater effects.

In Romans 6:1-4, in what are we united (identified) with Christ?

According to Romans 6:5-7, in what things are we united (identified) with Christ?

113

In Romans 6:8-11, in what are we united (identified) with Christ?

According to Ephesians 2:4-6, in what are we united (identified) with Christ?

Understand the Truth

Through the baptism of the Holy Spirit—of which water baptism is a picture—the Christian has been totally identified with Jesus Christ. We are united with Him in His death and burial (Romans 6:3), in His resurrection (Romans 6:4), and in His ascension (Ephesians 2:5-6). We are also united with Him in receiving new life (Romans 6:8). The Greek word translated "united" in Romans 6:5 literally means, "to make to grow together, to fuse." Being united with Christ, therefore, means that we become *fused together with Him.*

Consider items that are fused together such as fabrics or welded metal. The purpose of the fusing is usually to create something stronger, thicker, and holding together better than the original items. At our moment of fusing, we are no longer on our own, but Jesus' transforming life-giving power now lives in us. We are now connected to the King who has supreme power and authority. Our lives are stronger and fulfill a greater purpose than what we could have done before the fusing.

"Never think of yourself apart from Christ. (John Wesley, 18th century preacher)

We are continually **fused together** with Him and can live to enjoy the benefits of being **in Him**.

Reflect and Respond

Insert your name in the blanks below:

But because of His great love for _____, *God, who is*

rich in mercy, made _____ *alive with Christ even when*

you were dead in transgressions—it is by grace you have been saved. And God

raised _____ *up with Christ and seated*

_____ *with Him in the heavenly realms in Christ*

Jesus, (Ephesians 2:4-6).

Dwell on what it means to you to be fused with Christ.

THE BELIEVER'S IDENTITY IN CHRIST

Benefits of being identified with Christ

The moment you believed in Christ, the old self that was born **in Adam** died. A new self with the same body but a new interior started life as a new person with a new nature and a new inheritance. This radical new identity means you can never go back to not being **in Christ.** Ever!

Your new identity in Christ contains at least 35 characteristics or benefits. You get **all of these benefits at once**. God is not a vending machine, parceling out these benefits one at a time. Everything about our new identity and all the benefits are God's gift based on His love for you. You receive all of them at the moment of your salvation because you are **in Christ**. What God does to you is His choice, not yours. These benefits are **unconditional**. The burden of performance is upon God, not upon you.

These descriptions are true for every believer from the moment each person trusts in Jesus Christ for salvation. We will cover a few of them each day.

Read the Truth about Who You Are

ACCEPTED BY GOD

*Accept one another, then, **just as Christ accepted you**, in order to bring praise to God. (Romans 15:7)*

ADOPTED AS SONS AND HEIRS

*because those who are led by the Spirit of God **are sons of God**...you received the Spirit of **sonship**. And by Him, we cry out, 'Abba! Father!' (Romans 8:14-15)*

BAPTIZED INTO CHRIST'S BODY (THE CHURCH)

*For **we were all baptized by one Spirit into one body** —whether Jews or Greeks, slave or free — and we were all given the one Spirit to drink. (1 Corinthians 12:13)*

BORN AGAIN

*Praise be to the God and Father of our Lord Jesus Christ! In His great mercy, **He has given us new birth** into a living hope through the resurrection of Jesus Christ from the dead. (1 Peter 1:3)*

CHOSEN BY GOD

*For **He chose us in Him** before the creation of the world to be holy and blameless in His sight. (Ephesians 1:4)*

Reflect and Respond

Write a short description of your identity in Christ based on what you discovered in the verses you just read. "I am in Christ, ...

DAY 75

THE BELIEVER'S IDENTITY IN CHRIST

Read the Truth about Who You Are

CLOTHED WITH CHRIST

*For all of you who were baptized into Christ have **clothed yourselves with Christ**. (Galatians 3:27)*

FORGIVEN

*When you were dead in your sins and in the uncircumcision of your sinful nature, God made you alive with Christ. He **forgave us all our sins**, having cancelled the written code, with its regulations, that was against us and that stood opposed to us; He took it away, nailing it to the cross. (Colossians 2:13-14)*

FREED FROM CONDEMNATION (JUDGMENT)

*Therefore, there is now **no condemnation** for those who are in Christ Jesus. (Romans 8:1)*

__Whoever believes in him is not condemned__, but whoever does not believe stands condemned already because he has not believed in the name of God's one and only Son. (John 3:18)

FREED FROM THE LAW

*So my brothers, **you also died to the Law** through the body of Christ, that you might belong to another, to Him who was raised from the dead, that we might bear fruit to God. (Romans 7:4)*

FREE FROM GOD'S ANGER AGAINST SIN (PROPITIATION)

*"He is the **atoning sacrifice for our sins**, and not only for ours but also for the sins of the whole world." (1 John 2:2)*

Reflect and Respond

__Write a short description of your identity in Christ based on what you discovered in the verses you just read. "I am in Christ, …__

116

THE BELIEVER'S IDENTITY IN CHRIST

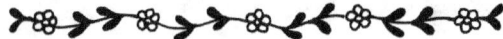

Read the Truth about Who You Are

GIVEN CHRIST'S RIGHTEOUSNESS

*God made Him who had no sin to be sin for us, so that **in Him we might become the righteousness of God**. (2 Corinthians 5:21)*

GIVEN CONFIDENT ACCESS TO GOD

*In Him and through faith in Him **we may approach God with freedom and confidence**. (Ephesians 3:12)*

*Therefore, brothers, since **we have confidence to enter the Most Holy Place** by the blood of Jesus, by a new and living way opened for us through the curtain, that is, His body, and since we have a great priest over the house of God, **let us draw near to God with a sincere heart in full assurance of faith**, having our hearts sprinkled to cleanse us from a guilty conscience and having our bodies washed with pure water. Let us hold unswervingly to the hope we profess, for He who promised is faithful. (Hebrews 10:19-23)*

GIVEN EVERY SPIRITUAL BLESSING

*Praise be the God and Father of our Lord Jesus Christ, who has blessed us in the heavenly realms with **every spiritual blessing** in Christ. (Ephesians 1:3)*

*His divine power has given us **everything we need for life and godliness** through our knowledge of Him who called us by His own glory and goodness. (2 Peter 1:3)*

GIVEN FULLNESS IN CHRIST

*For in Christ all the fullness of the Deity lives in bodily form, **you have been given fullness in Christ**... (Colossians 2:9-10)*

INDWELT BY THE HOLY SPIRIT

*You, however, are controlled not by the sinful nature but by the Spirit, if **the Spirit of God lives in you**. And if anyone does not have the Spirit of Christ, he does not belong to Christ. (Romans 8:9)*

Reflect and Respond

Write a short description of your identity in Christ based on what you discovered in the verses you just read. "I am in Christ, ...

The Believer's Identity in Christ

Read the Truth about Who You Are

JUSTIFIED (DECLARED RIGHTEOUS)

*For all have sinned and fall short of the glory of God, and are **justified freely by His grace** through the redemption that came by Christ Jesus. (Romans 3:23-24)*

MADE A NEW CREATION

*Therefore, if anyone is in Christ, **he is a new creation**; the old has gone, the new has come! (2 Corinthians 5:17)*

*For we are **God's workmanship, created in Christ Jesus** to do good works, which God prepared in advance for us to do. (Ephesians 2:10)*

MADE AT PEACE WITH GOD

*Therefore, since we have been justified by faith, **we have peace with God** through our Lord Jesus Christ. (Romans 5:1)*

MADE CHILDREN OF GOD

*Yet to all who received Him, to those who believed in His name, He gave the right to become **children of God**... (John 1:12)*

MADE CITIZENS OF HEAVEN

*But **our citizenship is in heaven**. And we eagerly await a Savior from there, the Lord Jesus Christ, who, by the power that enables Him to bring everything under His control, will transform our lowly bodies so that they will be like His glorious body. (Philippians 3:20-21)*

Reflect and Respond

Write a short description of your identity in Christ based on what you discovered in the verses you just read. "I am in Christ, …

THE BELIEVER'S IDENTITY IN CHRIST

Read the Truth about Who You Are

MADE HEIRS OF GOD

*Now if we are children, then **we are heirs — heirs of God and co-heirs with Christ**, if indeed we share in His sufferings in order that we may also share in His glory. (Rom. 8:17)*

*...since you are a son, **God has made you also an heir.** (Galatians 4:7)*

MADE HOLY AND BLAMELESS

*But now He has reconciled you by Christ's physical body through death to present you **holy in His sight, without blemish and free from accusation**... (Colossians 1:22)*

MADE INTO A HOLY AND ROYAL PRIESTHOOD

*To Him who loves us and has freed us from our sins by His blood, and has made us to be a **kingdom and priests to serve His God and Father...** (Revelation 1:5b-6)*

*You also, like living stones, are being built into a spiritual house to be a **holy priesthood, offering spiritual sacrifices** acceptable to God through Jesus Christ ... But you are a chosen people, a **royal priesthood**, a holy nation, a people belonging to God, that you may declare the praises of Him who called you out of darkness into His wonderful light. (1 Pet. 2:5,9)*

MADE INTO A TEMPLE OF THE HOLY SPIRIT

*Do you not know that **your body is a temple of the Holy Spirit**, who is in you, whom you have received from God? You are not your own? (1 Corinthians 6:19)*

MADE PERFECT FOREVER

*Because by one sacrifice He has **made perfect forever** those who are being made holy. (Hebrews 10:14)*

Reflect and Respond

Write a short description of your identity in Christ based on what you discovered in the verses you just read. "I am in Christ, ...

119

The Believer's Identity in Christ

Read the Truth about Who You Are

Never separated from God's Love

For I am convinced that neither death nor life, neither angels nor demons, neither the present nor the future, nor any powers, neither height nor depth, nor anything else in all creation, **will be able to separate us** *from the love of God that is in Christ Jesus our Lord. (Rom. 8:38-39)*

Reconciled to God

For if, when we were God's enemies, **we were reconciled to Him through the death of His Son***, how much more, having been reconciled, shall we be saved through His life. (Romans 5:10)*

Redeemed

In Him **we have redemption through His blood***, the forgiveness of sins, in accordance with the riches of God's grace. (Ephesians 1:7)*

Sanctified (made holy)

And by that will, **we have been made holy** *through the sacrifice of the body of Jesus Christ once for all. (Hebrews 10:10)*

And that is what some of you were. But you were washed, **you were sanctified***, you were justified in the name of the Lord Jesus Christ and by the Spirit of our God. (1 Corinthians 6:11)*

Safe from the wrath of God

Since we have now been justified by His blood, **how much more shall we be saved from God's wrath through Him***. (Romans 5:9)*

Reflect and Respond

Write a short description of your identity in Christ based on what you discovered in the verses you just read. "I am in Christ, …

THE BELIEVER'S IDENTITY IN CHRIST

Read the Truth about Who You Are

SAVED BY GRACE

*For it is **by grace you have been saved,** though faith — and this not from yourselves, it is the gift of God — not by works, so that no one can boast. (Ephesians 2:8-9)*

SEALED IN CHRIST

*And you also were included in Christ when you heard the word of truth... Having believed, **you were marked in Him with a seal, the promised Holy Spirit,** who is a deposit guaranteeing our inheritance until the redemption of those who are God's own possession — to the praise of His glory. (Ephesians 1:13-14)*

TRANSLATED OUT OF DARKNESS INTO LIGHT

*For you were once darkness, but **now you are light in the Lord.** Live as children of light. (Ephesians 5:8)*

TRANSLATED OUT OF DEATH INTO LIFE

*I tell you the truth, whoever hears my word and believes in Him who sent me **has eternal life** and will not be condemned; He **has crossed over from death into life.** (John 5:24)*

*As for you, you were **dead** in your transgressions and sins...But because of His great love for us, God, who is rich in mercy, **made us alive with Christ** even when we were **dead** in transgressions... (Ephesians 2:1,4-5)*

WASHED CLEAN

*And that is what some of you were. But **you were washed,** you were sanctified, you were justified in the name of the Lord Jesus Christ and by the Spirit of our God. (1 Corinthians 6:11)*

Reflect and Respond

Write a short description of your identity in Christ based on what you discovered in the verses you just read. "I am in Christ, ...

DAY 81

FREEDOM OF YOUR NEW IDENTITY

Knowing your identity sets you free from the world's viewpoint.

As stated before, the world isn't going to validate your new identity. From a worldly point of view, you are viewed as the same you've always been—with the baggage still hanging around your neck. But you can know your true identity—what God has done to change you from the inside out. And knowing that sets you free from the world's constraints and expectations, from your past, and from the garbage that others feed you about your failures.

> "Some of us are drawn in by circumstance [wearing ourselves out by our own efforts] because we don't know who we are. The greatest crisis is not outside; it's the identity crisis within those of the faith! Men and women of God are so focused on the darkness that they're missing the adventure." (Michelle Wallace, "Fruit of the Vine: The Greatness of God," *Living Magazine,* October 2012)

Read the Truth about Who You Are

The chart below contrasts the world's **lies** about who you are with the FACT of God's **truth** about who you are.

The World's Lies (are)	*God's Truth (says)*
You are still a sinner because you sometimes sin.	You are a saint (one declared righteous by God) who sometimes sins.
You get your identity from what you have done.	You get your identity from what God has done for you.
You get your identity from what people say about you.	You get your identity from what God says about you.
Your behavior tells you what to believe about yourself.	Your belief about yourself directs your behavior.

(Adapted from Dr. Timothy Warner, *Resolving Spiritual Conflicts and Cross-Cultural Ministry,* Freedom in Christ Ministries, 1993.)

Reflect and Respond

One of the fundamental questions of the human race is that of identity, "Who am I?" The one secure, eternal answer is that through faith in Jesus Christ you can say, "I am in Christ, a child of God, one of God's saints, totally loved and accepted by God"—an identity that no circumstance can change!

Respond through any means you choose (journaling, prayer, poem, art, song) to illustrate what you have learned about your identity in Christ.

part 7

GRACE-BASED FREEDOM

The only thing I want to learn from you is this: Did you receive the Spirit by doing the works of the law or by believing what you heard? Are you so foolish? Although you began with the Spirit, are you now trying to finish by human effort? Have you suffered so many things for nothing? – if indeed it was for nothing. Does God then give you the Spirit and work miracles among you by your doing the works of the law or by your believing what you heard? (Galatians 3:2-5)

Introduction to Law and Grace

Read the Truth

² I would like to learn just one thing from you: Did you receive the Spirit by the works of the law, or by believing what you heard? ³ Are you so foolish? After beginning by means of the Spirit, are you now trying to finish by means of the flesh? ⁴ Have you experienced so much in vain—if it really was in vain? ⁵ So again I ask, does God give you His Spirit and work miracles among you by the works of the law, or by your believing what you heard? (GALATIANS 3:2-5)

Confirm the Truth

What did Paul ask the Galatians about how they received the Spirit in Galatians 3:2?

After beginning by means of the Spirit, what are they doing now (Galatians 3:3)?

What question did Paul ask them in Galatians 3:5?

Understand the Truth

You have a great foundation now, knowing what Christ has done on the cross for you and how His resurrection provides the means for you to receive a new life with a new identity. Praise God for His indescribable gift!

But as seen in the Galatians 3 scripture quoted above, many Christians start out accepting the gift of salvation but then are thrown into a *works-related* way of living out this new life in order to maintain acceptance before a holy God. The issue is broadly called "Law and Grace." Understanding the difference between these two concepts is the foundation of the gospel of Jesus Christ and the basis for experiencing a joyful Christian life.

Understanding the difference between Law and Grace answers important biblical questions:

1. What is the difference between the Old and New Testaments? What Old Testament promises can be claimed by New Testament believers?
2. What must we do to be saved or to even stay saved?

124

3. Where do we fit in God's plan of history? What should we expect from God and from life in this phase?

The most important question, however, is this, "How are we to live to please God?" Understanding the difference between Law and Grace answers questions about three specific areas of the Christian life:

- Our **motivation** for Christian living—Is our motivation to live the Christian life based on love and gratitude for what Christ has done for us, or is it based on fear of what God will do to us every time we fail?

- Our **power** for Christian living—Do we think the power to live the Christian life is self-generated or Spirit-empowered? Through self-effort or through dying to self?

- Our **relationships**—We often treat others the same way we think God treats us. If we think of God as mean and spiteful, we will often relate to others that way. Are we trying to motivate others to obedience through fear of punishment—given out by God or by us?

Reflect and Respond

Probably the simplest way to understand Law and Grace is to see it as the issue of God's acceptance: "On what basis is a person made acceptable before a holy God?"

Based upon what you've learned so far, how would you answer that question?

125

What is "The Law?"

>❀ ❀ ❀ ❀ ❀ ❀ ❀<

Reading through the New Testament, you will often see this phrase mentioned—"the Law" (not always capitalized in English translations). Generally, the New Testament writers mean "the Mosaic Law" by this phrase. The Mosaic Law is, "The covenant between God and the nation of Israel instituted at Mt. Sinai after the Exodus from Egypt." Let's gain some perspective on this.

Read the Truth

The Lord had said to Abram, "Go from your country, your people and your father's household to the land I will show you. I will make you into a great nation, and I will bless you; I will make your name great, and you will be a blessing. I will bless those who bless you, and whoever curses you I will curse; and all peoples on earth will be blessed through you." (Genesis 12:1-3)

See, I have taught you decrees and laws as the Lord my God commanded me, so that you may follow them in the land you are entering to take possession of it. Observe them carefully, for this will show your wisdom and understanding to the nations, who will hear about all these decrees and say, "Surely this great nation is a wise and understanding people." What other nation is so great as to have their gods near them the way the Lord our God is near us whenever we pray to Him? And what other nation is so great as to have such righteous decrees and laws as this body of laws I am setting before you today? (Deuteronomy 4:5-8)

Confirm the Truth

What did God promise to Abraham in Genesis 12:1-3?

According to Deuteronomy 4:5-8, what was the purpose of the Law?

Understand the Truth

In Genesis 12:1-3, God promised to Abraham that He would make Abraham into a great nation and that all the peoples on earth would be blessed through Abraham. Abraham's descendants multiplied greatly while living in Egypt, and God delivered them out of Egypt to form the nation He had promised to Abraham. At Mt. Sinai, God proposed a contractual agreement (the Law) to the new nation (Exodus 19:3-6). After God spoke the outline of the Law (the Ten Commandments) and the provisions of the Law to the people (Exodus 20-23), the nation agreed to keep the contract (Exodus 24:3-8).

From the simplest, big-picture point of view, the Law of Moses [Mosaic Law, hereafter designated as the Law] described the conditions under which: 1) Israel would be allowed to dwell in the promised land; and 2) the people of

126

Israel would enjoy the presence of God dwelling in their midst. The Law was bilateral (two-sided), meaning that God offered earthly blessings for obedience and earthly curses for disobedience (Deuteronomy 28). The Law was not a means of salvation. The Law was primarily *national* in scope and *earthly* in application.

The nation of Israel was to be a holy nation as God was a holy God. "**Be holy** because I, the LORD your God, am holy" (Leviticus 19:2). For a person to be holy required separation from sin. So much of the Law includes animal sacrifices for the sin of the people so God could remove their sins from them (Leviticus 16:20-22), making them holy again. The Law was a separate arrangement for a temporary purpose. It was for managing sinful people until its fulfillment in Christ.

Reflect and Respond

127

DAY 84

WHAT IS "THE LAW?"

Read the Truth

We know that the law is good if one uses it properly. We also know that the law is made not for the righteous but for lawbreakers and rebels, the ungodly and sinful, the unholy and irreligious, for those who kill their fathers or mothers, for murderers, for the sexually immoral, for those practicing homosexuality, for slave traders and liars and perjurers—and for whatever else is contrary to the sound doctrine. (1 Timothy 1:8-10)

Why, then, was the law given at all? It was added because of transgressions until the Seed to whom the promise referred had come. The law was given through angels and entrusted to a mediator. A mediator, however, implies more than one party; but God is one. Is the law, therefore, opposed to the promises of God? Absolutely not! For if a law had been given that could impart life, then righteousness would certainly have come by the law. But Scripture has locked up everything under the control of sin, so that what was promised, being given through faith in Jesus Christ, might be given to those who believe. Before the coming of this faith, we were held in custody under the law, locked up until the faith that was to come would be revealed. So the law was our guardian until Christ came that we might be justified by faith. Now that this faith has come, we are no longer under a guardian. So in Christ Jesus you are all children of God through faith, (Galatians 3:19-26)

Confirm the Truth

What did Paul say was the purpose of the Law (1 Timothy 1:8-10)?

What did not come by the Law (Galatians 3:19-26)?

What was the intended duration for the Law (Galatians 3:19-26)?

What did the Law do until that time?

128

Understand the Truth

The purpose of the Law was to teach central truths about God. There had to be a nation on earth that knew something about God to teach the rest of the world (Deuteronomy 4:5-8). The purpose of the Law was also protective to preserve Israel as a distinct people through whom the promised Messiah would come to bless the whole world. The Law would also help to stop the sinful by identifying the lawbreakers, rebels and ungodly.

Eventually, the Law would lead people to a trust relationship with the Lord by showing them their sin and leaving faith—trusting in the mercy and grace of God alone to forgive one's guilt—as the only way to be right with God. This prepared the way for the work of Christ. The Law could not impart life (Galatians 3:21) or righteousness. Salvation and spiritual life for Old Testament believers came through **faith in a merciful God**.

Reflect and Respond

THE NEW COVENANT

❦❦❦❦❦❦❦❦❦❦❦❦

Because the Law had limitations, God promised a New Covenant. The Jews knew about the New Covenant God promised in Jeremiah 31:31-34. When Jesus spoke about the New Covenant the night before He died, this is what He was referencing. Hebrews 8:8-12 quotes Jeremiah 31:31-34.

Read the Truth

7 For if there had been nothing wrong with that first covenant, no place would have been sought for another. 8 But God found fault with the people and said: "The days are coming, declares the Lord, when I will make a new covenant with the people of Israel and with the people of Judah. 9 It will not be like the covenant I made with their ancestors when I took them by the hand to lead them out of Egypt, because they did not remain faithful to my covenant, and I turned away from them, declares the Lord. 10 This is the covenant I will establish with the people of Israel after that time, declares the Lord. I will put my laws in their minds and write them on their hearts. I will be their God, and they will be my people. 11 No longer will they teach their neighbor, or say to one another, 'Know the Lord,' because they will all know me, from the least of them to the greatest. 12 For I will forgive their wickedness and will remember their sins no more." 13 By calling this covenant "new," He has made the first one obsolete; and what is obsolete and outdated will soon disappear. (Hebrews 8:7-13)

Confirm the Truth

Why did God make a New Covenant according to Hebrews 8:7-9?

Based on verses 10-12, why would the New Covenant be better?

What would happen to the Old Covenant (verse 13)?

Understand the Truth

Because believers have a change of heart and the Holy Spirit's presence inside, the motivation to please God is internal rather than external as with the Law. This promotes transparency in our relationship with God and helps us to obey our God better. Our acceptance before God is not based on our never messing up. It is God's choice to hold onto us because we are in Christ. Under this New Covenant, we get to know God personally regardless of our status in life because our relationship with God is based upon our faith in Jesus Christ. And our sins are not just covered but are taken away forever.

Under the Law (Old Covenant), blessings were *conditional* and the burden of performance was on *people*. Under the New Covenant, the promised blessings are *unconditional* and the burden of performance is upon *God*. Our sole responsibility toward the fulfillment of the New Covenant is to enter into that relationship through faith in Jesus Christ. Then, **God commits Himself to complete** the work He began in us (Philippians 1:6) until we are conformed to the image of His Son (Romans 8:29). This doesn't mean that Christians have no responsibilities at all! We are called to follow Jesus Christ diligently and live worthy of our calling (Ephesians 4:1).

Reflect and Respond

131

DAY 86

THE PROBLEM OF GALATIANISM

Read the Truth

I would like to learn just one thing from you: Did you receive the Spirit by the works of the law, or by believing what you heard? Are you so foolish? After beginning by means of the Spirit, are you now trying to finish by means of the flesh? Have you experienced so much in vain—if it really was in vain? So again I ask, does God give you His Spirit and work miracles among you by the works of the law, or by your believing what you heard? (Galatians 3:2-5)

Certain people came down from Judea to Antioch and were teaching the believers: "Unless you are circumcised, according to the custom taught by Moses, you cannot be saved." This brought Paul and Barnabas into sharp dispute and debate with them. So Paul and Barnabas were appointed, along with some other believers, to go up to Jerusalem to see the apostles and elders about this question. The church sent them on their way, and as they traveled through Phoenicia and Samaria, they told how the Gentiles had been converted. This news made all the believers very glad. When they came to Jerusalem, they were welcomed by the church and the apostles and elders, to whom they reported everything God had done through them. Then some of the believers who belonged to the party of the Pharisees stood up and said, "The Gentiles must be circumcised and required to keep the Law of Moses." (Acts 15:1-5)

Confirm the Truth

What problem did Paul address in Galatians 3:2-5?

What were the Judaizers teaching (Acts 15:1-5)?

Understand the Truth

God's plan is too easy for many to accept. And old habits of performance-based religion are hard to die. That's what Paul was talking about in Galatians 3:2-5, and the problem came to be called "Galatianism."

The term "Galatianism" developed because of issues addressed in Paul's letter to the Galatians—believers in several churches in the area of what is now central Turkey. As recorded in Acts 13-14, Paul and Barnabas spread the gospel in this area on their first missionary journey about 15 years after Jesus' death and resurrection. The Galatian churches were composed of mostly Gentile (non-Jewish) believers. Many of the Jews in the region rejected the preaching of Paul about Christ's death and resurrection. They did not respond with faith in Jesus Christ in order to receive eternal life (Acts 13:46). The Gentiles, however, were "glad and honored the word of the Lord" (Acts 13:47-48). After Paul left the area, some unnamed teachers (usually called "Judaizers" in the Bible) followed in his wake, contradicting his

132

teachings. Eventually the controversy grew so heated that it was brought to Jerusalem to be decided by the apostles.

The Judaizers' solution was basically: "We have the promises, Christ, and salvation. If you want them, you must come over to our side." In their worldview, the Gentiles must become Jews first, start obeying the Mosaic Law, then they could be acceptable to God and receive salvation through faith in Christ. Gentiles had joined the Jewish faith that way in the Old Testament. The Judaizers thought it still worked that way. But God had a new plan and a different goal.

Reflect and Respond

DAY 87

THE PROBLEM OF GALATIANISM

Read the Truth

Therefore, remember that formerly you who are Gentiles by birth and called "uncircumcised" by those who call themselves "the circumcision" (which is done in the body by human hands)— remember that at that time you were separate from Christ, excluded from citizenship in Israel and foreigners to the covenants of the promise, without hope and without God in the world. (Ephesians 2:11-12)

13 But now in Christ Jesus you who once were far away have been brought near by the blood of Christ. 14 For He Himself is our peace, who has made the two groups one and has destroyed the barrier, the dividing wall of hostility, 15 by setting aside in His flesh the Law with its commands and regulations. His purpose was to create in Himself one new humanity out of the two, thus making peace,16 and in one body to reconcile both of them to God through the cross, by which He put to death their hostility. (Ephesians 2:13-16)

17 He came and preached peace to you who were far away and peace to those who were near. 18 For through Him we both have access to the Father by one Spirit. 19 Consequently, you are no longer foreigners and strangers, but fellow citizens with God's people and also members of His household, 20 built on the foundation of the apostles and prophets, with Christ Jesus Himself as the chief cornerstone. 21 In Him the whole building is joined together and rises to become a holy temple in the Lord. 22 And in Him you too are being built together to become a dwelling in which God lives by His Spirit. (Ephesians 2:17-22)

In reading this, then, you will be able to understand my insight into the mystery of Christ, which was not made known to people in other generations as it has now been revealed by the Spirit to God's holy apostles and prophets. This mystery is that through the gospel the Gentiles are heirs together with Israel, members together of one body, and sharers together in the promise in Christ Jesus. (Ephesians 3:4-6)

Confirm the Truth

What was the condition of the Gentiles before hearing of Christ (Ephesians 2:11-12)?

In Ephesians 2:14, Christ made the two groups (Jews and Gentiles) into one by breaking down the barrier of the dividing wall. What was the dividing wall (the first part of verse 15)?

What was Christ's purpose according to Ephesians 2:15-16?

What are the results of this barrier coming down according to Ephesians 2:18-20?

What was the mystery of Christ unknown to the Jews in the past but now being revealed (Ephesians 3:4-6)?

Understand the Truth

In Ephesians, Paul described the state of the Gentiles (non-Jews who represented the world in general) as separate from Christ, excluded from citizenship with God's people, foreigners to the promise of God, without hope and without God. The Jews looked upon them as uncircumcised sinners. The Judaizers' solution was basically: "We have the promises, Christ, and salvation. If you want them, you must come over to our side." But God had a new plan and a different goal.

God's goal in the New Covenant is to make both groups into one (Ephesians 2:14). The Gentiles and the Jews would join the Church ("one new humanity out of the two") as equals and co-heirs of everything promised by God to all those who believe in Jesus Christ. Christ broke down the dividing wall, the Law with its commandments and regulations, that separated the Jews from the Gentiles. The barrier had to come down so that Christ could create in Himself a new humanity out of the two groups. He would reconcile both groups to God through the cross, not through the Law. As a result, there is peace between Jew and Gentile in Christ. Both have access to the Father by one Spirit. Both share together all the promises in Jesus Christ.

It is important to remember that the Mosaic Law was a covenant **between God and the nation Israel only**. At no time was it imposed on other nations of the world. While the Old Testament frequently describes prophetically the blessings the whole world will receive through the Messiah (Christ) and His kingdom, there was a great secret (a "mystery") held in the heart of God. That mystery was that the Gentiles, who were held separate from the Jews by the Law, would be included in God's promises through the gospel of Jesus Christ. The mystery is now revealed. To God be the glory!

Reflect and Respond

THE PROBLEM OF GALATIANISM

Read the Truth

When you were dead in your sins and in the uncircumcision of your flesh, God made you alive with Christ. He forgave us all our sins, having canceled the charge of our legal indebtedness, which stood against us and condemned us; He has taken it away, nailing it to the cross. (Colossians 2:13-14)

For sin shall no longer be your master, because you are not under the Law, but under grace. (Romans 6:14)

So my brothers and sisters, you also died to the Law through the body of Christ, that you might belong to another, to Him who was raised from the dead, in order that we might bear fruit for God. For when we were in the realm of the flesh, the sinful passions aroused by the law were at work in us, so that we bore fruit for death. But now, by dying to what once bound us, we have been released from the Law so that we serve in the new way of the Spirit, and not in the old way of the written code. (Romans 7:4-6)

The apostles and elders met to consider this question. After much discussion, Peter got up and addressed them: "Brothers, you know that some time ago God made a choice among you that the Gentiles might hear from my lips the message of the gospel and believe. God, who knows the heart, showed that He accepted them by giving the Holy Spirit to them, just as He did to us. He did not discriminate between us and them, for He purified their hearts by faith. Now then, why do you try to test God by putting on the necks of Gentiles a yoke that neither we nor our ancestors have been able to bear? No! We believe it is through the grace of our Lord Jesus that we are saved, just as they are." (Acts 15:6-11)

Confirm the Truth

According to Colossians 2:13-14, what happened to the Law ("our legal indebtedness")?

What is the Christian's relation to the Law now (Romans 6:14)?

What is the Christian's relation to the Law now (Romans 7:4-6)?

136

After open debate, the apostles under the inspiration of the Holy Spirit gave an answer to the Judaizers' position (Acts 15:1-5). What did the apostles conclude in Acts 15:6-11?

Understand the Truth

The Law, the legal indebtedness that stood against us, was nailed to the cross. It was canceled. The word Paul used there meant destroyed, wiped away, erased, and blotted out. That sounds pretty permanent, doesn't it? Romans 6 and 7 plainly declare that Christians are not under the Law, are dead to the Law and are released from the Law. Released. The Law no longer comes into play regarding our living a life that pleases God. This is crucial to *graceful living!*

The apostolic council's decision confirmed this based on Peter's testimony of what he saw with his own eyes. The Gentiles and Jews are equally saved by faith in Christ alone and equally given the full blessings of salvation. The Law is no longer needed. It was a burdensome yoke upon the Jews for so many years. God's new plan was so much better!

Reflect and Respond

DAY 89

THE PROBLEM OF GALATIANISM

Read the Truth

I am astonished that you are so quickly deserting the one who called you to live in the grace of Christ and are turning to a different gospel—which is really no gospel at all. Evidently some people are throwing you into confusion and are trying to pervert the gospel of Christ. But even if we or an angel from heaven should preach a gospel other than the one we preached to you, let them be under God's curse! As we have already said, so now I say again: If anybody is preaching to you a gospel other than what you accepted, let them be under God's curse! (Galatians 1:6-9)

You foolish Galatians! Who has bewitched you? Before your very eyes Jesus Christ was clearly portrayed as crucified. I would like to learn just one thing from you: Did you receive the Spirit by the works of the Law, or by believing what you heard? Are you so foolish? After beginning by means of the Spirit, are you now trying to finish by means of the flesh? Have you experienced so much in vain—if it really was in vain? So again I ask, does God give you His Spirit and work miracles among you by the works of the Law, or by your believing what you heard? (Galatians 3:1-5)

It is for freedom that Christ has set us free. Stand firm, then, and do not let yourselves be burdened again by a yoke of slavery. Mark my words! I, Paul, tell you that if you let yourselves be circumcised, Christ will be of no value to you at all. Again I declare to every man who lets himself be circumcised that he is obligated to obey the whole Law. (Galatians 5:1-3)

Confirm the Truth

The book of Galatians as a whole was written to address the panic created by the Judaizers' teaching. Yet, the warnings and truths are applicable to anyone today who thinks you have to follow the Law to be true Christians.

What does Paul say that the Galatians are deserting in Galatians 1:6-9?

What is the answer to the question Paul asks three times in Galatians 3:1-5 to bring the readers back to the truth?

What does Paul say they should do and should not do (Galatians 5:1-3)?

138

It is for what that Christ has set us free?

Understand the Truth

Paul responded with conviction to anyone who thinks they must follow the Law to be true Christians. Following that kind of teaching is desertion of the gospel and no gospel at all. It is opposite of what the gospel teaches. God works in us through His Spirit and by faith. Don't let anyone put you in that slavery again. Instead, live in your freedom through the Spirit. Live out your life based on grace.

So if Christians are no longer under the Law of Moses in any way, shape or form, why read and study the Old Testament? Paul anticipates our question when he writes this,

"All Scripture is God-breathed and is useful for teaching, rebuking, correcting and training in righteousness, so that the man of God may be thoroughly equipped for every good work." (2 Timothy 3:16-17)

When Paul wrote those words under the guidance of the Holy Spirit, ALL Scripture at that time was the whole Old Testament. God has revealed Himself through what is written—His holiness, goodness, sovereignty, omniscience, omnipotence, love and more. For the people of Israel (and for Gentile converts who voluntarily took on the yoke of the Law), the Law served as their rule of life—**learning to approach life God's way**. The Law God gave to Israel included 3 sections: civil (how to govern the nation), religious (how to worship a holy God), and moral (how to treat one another). Though Christians are not under the civil or religious laws, God's moral law has not changed and is reinforced in New Testament writings. So…

The Law can be *properly* used as a **lens** through which to see the perfect character and righteousness of God. Yet, Jesus Christ is an even greater revelation of God (John 1:17-18; 14:5-8). The Law can also be properly used as a **mirror** in which to see oneself truly in comparison to the righteousness of God, especially the moral law (dealing with murder, marriage, relationships, etc.). The Law can't clean you up, but it can reveal that you have a problem (Romans 3:19-20; 1 Timothy 1:8-10). The Law is *improperly* used as a ladder on which to climb up to try to earn the acceptance of God.

By the time of Jesus, rabbis taught that the whole Law could be summed up with two sentences,

"…Love the Lord your God with all your heart and with all your soul and with all your strength and with all your mind'; and, 'Love your neighbor as yourself." (Luke 10:27)

That hasn't changed. And the rest of the New Testament describes how to live that way.

Reflect and Respond

Based upon what you just learned, posting "The Ten Commandments" from Exodus 20 as your rule of life might give the wrong message to other believers or to the unbelieving world. Consider some New Testament verses that would be far more effective in communicating God's grace to an unbelieving world than posting the "Ten Commandments" (the Law given to Israel).

DAY 90

THE TENDENCY TOWARD LEGALISM

You may be thinking, "What does Galatianism have to do with me?" Be aware that Galatianism is still present in the modern church. We call it "legalism" (legal = relating to the law). Legalism is not about what is clearly taught as right and wrong from God's perspective in Scripture, that which God calls "sin." Legalism **is the addition of any other conditions to faith in order to gain and maintain acceptance from God.**

Read the Truth

Therefore do not let anyone judge you by what you eat or drink, or with regard to a religious festival, a New Moon celebration or a Sabbath day. These are a shadow of the things that were to come; the reality, however, is found in Christ. Do not let anyone who delights in false humility and the worship of angels disqualify you. Such a person also goes into great detail about what they have seen; they are puffed up with idle notions by their unspiritual mind. They have lost connection with the head, from whom the whole body, supported and held together by its ligaments and sinews, grows as God causes it to grow. (Colossians 2:16-19)

Since you died with Christ to the elemental spiritual forces of this world, why, as though you still belonged to the world, do you submit to its rules: "Do not handle! Do not taste! Do not touch!"? These rules, which have to do with things that are all destined to perish with use, are based on merely human commands and teachings. Such regulations indeed have an appearance of wisdom, with their self-imposed worship, their false humility and their harsh treatment of the body, but they lack any value in restraining sensual indulgence. (Colossians 2:20-23)

Confirm the Truth

What warnings did Paul give in Colossians 2:16-19?

Rather than producing righteousness, what can legalism produce or not produce (Colossians 2:20-23)?

Understand the Truth

At this point, we move our attention from the Law as referring to the Law of Moses, including the Ten Commandments, and all the statutes and ordinances (found in Exodus, Leviticus, Numbers and Deuteronomy) to law as a principle. Living by *law* can be **any man-made system of works by which a person attempts to approach God on her own merits or performance.** That's what legalism does.

Paul warned the Colossians about legalistic practices and thinking that could affect their lives. Those included what one eats or drinks, participation in religious festivals, and Sabbath requirements. He also mentioned anything

140

that gives someone false humility and worship or focus on spiritual beings such as angels. Those experiences lead to arrogance and pride (being puffed up) and take your focus away from Christ. Continuing his discussion of living by the law (do not handle, taste or touch), Paul points out the fact that those activities only lead to an appearance of wisdom. Such outward conformity generates pride and lacks any value in controlling sinful sensual lusts.

Modern examples of legalism are rules that require you to listen to only certain kinds of music and not wear certain types of clothing. Legalism makes rules for when and how often you must attend church and what you are allowed to eat and drink to stay acceptable to God. Legalism declares certain activities sinful when God doesn't. Following such "checklists" can cause boasting and a hardened heart toward others who do not abide by such rules.

Reflect and Respond

Do you recognize any tendencies toward legalism or the influence of legalism in your own life? What "faith plus _____" teaching has influenced your life? Or what manmade rules have you been taught to obey to remain acceptable to God?

THE TENDENCY TOWARD LEGALISM

Read the Truth

For it is by grace you have been saved, through faith—and this is not from yourselves, it is the gift of God—not by works, so that no one can boast. (Ephesians 2:8-9)

You who are trying to be justified by the law have been alienated from Christ; you have fallen away from grace. For through the Spirit we eagerly await by faith the righteousness for which we hope. For in Christ Jesus neither circumcision nor uncircumcision has any value. The only thing that counts is faith expressing itself through love. (Galatians 5:4-6)

Confirm the Truth

Why did God choose to give us salvation by His grace based on our faith alone (Ephesians 2:8-9)?

What does Paul say about those trying to be justified by the Law in Galatians 5:4?

Understand the Truth

Legalism is the addition of any other conditions to faith in order to gain and maintain acceptance from God. One example is the insistence of "faith plus _____" in order to maintain good standing with God. This legalism teaches that you must have **faith plus** other evidences: good works, refraining from certain sins, church membership, ordinances or sacraments (baptism, communion), or paying a penalty/penance for sin. **Whenever God's acceptance of you has an "IF" attached to it (other than faith in Jesus Christ), you know you are in the vicinity of legalism.**

Another example involves repentance. Repentance means a change of mind. True repentance for the unbeliever is changing your mind regarding your sin (recognize that it separates you from God) and regarding Christ (recognize that He alone is the answer to your sin problem) and then trusting in Him for salvation. Legalism teaches that repentance means you have to give up your sins before Christ will accept you and give you salvation.

Legalism leads to a dramatically different experience of Christian living. Many groups or individuals begin with a clear presentation of the gospel of grace to receive salvation, then proceed to live by works, trying to earn or maintain God's acceptance by performance (as in Galatians 3:2-5).

Whether a person is trying to live by (1) the God-given Mosaic Law (particularly the 10 Commandments), (2) by human laws imposed by others (standards of what they consider spiritual and necessary to please God and/or prove you are saved), or even (3) by self-imposed laws, the effects on the individual are the same: fear, guilt, and condemnation.

A person is "living according to law" (legalism) whenever she tries to approach God on the basis of her own merits or performance. Though the outward effects are often subtle, a believer trying to live by legalism will actually be drifting her focus away from the person and work of Jesus Christ. She is straying from **enjoying a relationship to practicing a religion.** In Galatians 5:4, Paul calls this "have fallen away from grace." Based upon all that we have learned so far about a believer's permanent identity in Christ, the phrase "falling away from grace" cannot mean losing one's salvation. Considering the problem that Paul is addressing in Galatians, it is referring to that drifting away from relying solely on the person and work of Jesus Christ to maintain your acceptance before God.

But God's plan leaves no room for anyone to boast about their works or claim for themselves that they worked for their salvation (Ephesians 2:8-9).

Reflect and Respond

If you have been taught any "faith plus any other condition" in order to maintain acceptance to God, get to heaven, or get any other blessing (which you already have in Christ!), consider how this has affected your life, your emotions, your thinking, or your relationship with God and others. Then, let it go and cling to the truth of your identity in Christ.

DAY 92

THE TENDENCY TOWARD LEGALISM

Read the Truth

Now to the one who works, wages are not credited as a gift but as an obligation. However, to the one who does not work but trusts God who justifies the ungodly, their faith is credited as righteousness. (Romans 4:4-5)

So too, at the present time there is a remnant chosen by grace. And if by grace, then it cannot be based on works; if it were, grace would no longer be grace. (Romans 11:5-6)

So also Abraham "believed God, and it was credited to him as righteousness." (Galatians 3:6)

Brothers and sisters, let me take an example from everyday life. Just as no one can set aside or add to a human covenant that has been duly established, so it is in this case. The promises were spoken to Abraham and to his seed. Scripture does not say "and to seeds," meaning many people, but "and to your seed" meaning one person, who is Christ. What I mean is this: The law, introduced 430 years later, does not set aside the covenant previously established by God and thus do away with the promise. For if the inheritance depends on the Law, then it no longer depends on the promise; but God in His grace gave it to Abraham through a promise. (Galatians 3:15-18)

Confirm the Truth

What example does Paul give to show why law and grace are incompatible in Romans 4:4-5?

According to Romans 11:5-6, why can law and grace not co-exist?

By what did Abraham receive righteousness from God—his faith or his works (Galatians 3:6)?

What did God confirm through Paul about the timing of His covenant of grace in relation to the Law (Galatians 3:15-18)?

Understand the Truth

To show why law and grace are incompatible, Paul used the illustration of work in Romans 4:4-5. A worker expects wages, which are a reward for his work. The one not working must trust God to receive righteousness, the reward for faith. In Romans 11:6, Paul declares that works nullify the benefits of grace. This is not referring to salvation but to enjoying the benefits of everything that grace gives to the Christian based on her faith. And God gave His promise of salvation based on faith. Abraham was declared righteous by faith alone 430 years before the Law was given. God's determination of righteousness by faith through His grace alone came before the Law.

Out of God's mercy comes His **grace**. Remember that grace is unmerited favor. It is a gift that is undeserved. Grace is a gift God chooses to give because of His great love and mercy, apart from the law (Romans 3:21). Law (Mosaic or human-imposed religious standards) is incompatible with "Grace!" Like Jesus' example of pouring new wine into new wineskins rather than into old ones (Matthew 9:14-17), grace cannot be added to the law. It is one or the other. You cannot accept both.

Reflect and Respond

Considering the eventual results of being influenced by either law or grace, which one would you rather guide the course of your life?

THE DIFFERENCE BETWEEN PUNISHMENT AND DISCIPLINE

Part 1: "Law" motivates us to obedience by fear of punishment

The issue of "Law and Grace" often arises because of two reasons: 1) the tendency to think you can control sin through lots of rules and 2) the tendency to interpret events. Let's explore the second reason some more.

Everyone must deal with disappointments, problems, and tragedies in life. The human tendency is to try to interpret events as *signs* of God's anger or favor, asking questions such as: *"Why did this happen? What does it mean? What is God trying to tell me?"* Through this tendency, people (even Christians) lapse into thinking that God is angry with them because they must have done something wrong. Otherwise, why would they suffer?

Professing Christians may acknowledge grace as true but live as though their own performance of religious standards determines their fate in life. They live in fear of God, not a healthy fear, but an unhealthy one—a fear of what God will do to them every time they fail. That becomes the motivation for their Christian living. Why do some believers succumb to this thinking? The answer is that we probably don't understand the difference between *punishment* and *discipline.*

- Punishment is a penalty imposed on an offender for a crime or wrongdoing. Punishment is backward- looking toward the offense, impersonal, and chiefly concerned with "balancing the books of justice." Its primary concern is not correcting future behavior. Example: getting a speeding ticket.

- Discipline is training that develops character, self-control, orderliness and/or efficiency. It is forward-looking to a change of behavior and/or character, is individually tailored, personally applied, and is chiefly concerned with what will benefit the individual in question. Discipline is **not** always corrective or applied in response to sin; it is **ongoing**. Think "training." Example: learning to brush teeth.

Punishment and discipline sometimes look alike (especially to the one on the receiving end). But the difference can be seen in both the attitude and the goal of the one applying them. The attitude behind punishment is **anger** and **indignation**, and the goal is **justice.** The attitude behind discipline is **love**, and the goal is the **development** of the person. You can probably think of a time or two when you have confused these two concepts in your life. Now, let's see what the Bible says.

Read the Truth

Since we have now been justified by His blood, how much more shall we be saved from God's wrath through Him! (Romans 5:9)

Therefore, there is now no condemnation for those who are in Christ Jesus, because through Christ Jesus the law of the Spirit who gives life has set you free from the law of sin and death. (Romans 8:1-2)

This is how love is made complete among us so that we will have confidence on the day of judgment: In this world we are like Jesus. There is no fear in love. But perfect love drives out fear, because fear has to do with punishment. The one who fears is not made perfect in love. We love because He first loved us. (1 John 4:17-19)

Those whom I love I rebuke and discipline. So be earnest and repent. (Revelation 3:19)

Confirm the Truth

What does Romans 5:9 declare to you about freedom from punishment?

What do Romans 8:1-2 declare to you about freedom from punishment?

What further confidence do we gain from 1 John 4:17-19?

What does God declare in Revelation 3:19 about disciplining His own?

Understand the Truth

In Christ, we are saved from God's wrath against sin and rebellion against Him. There is no condemnation for us! According to 1 John 4, we are made perfect in God's love so we should not fear God and not expect Him to punish us on the day of judgment. Our salvation delivers us from that punishment. The Bible teaches that every believer will be judged at the *"Judgment Seat of Christ"* (2 Corinthians 5:10). This, however, is not a *criminal trial* where the fate of the defendant is in question, nor his guilt or innocence. It is an *evaluation* for the purpose of rewards (1Corinthians 3:11-15). Believers are already declared not guilty of sin…in Christ…forever!

Yet, for those He loves, God will discipline (train) us to choose the right way of approaching life over the wrong way. Under the grace of the New Covenant, believers are disciplined (trained), not punished. God's discipline stems from His love (Revelation 3:19). Confidence in His love for you should cast out any fear of punishment that you may have. Erase it from your memory banks.

Reflect and Respond

In what areas of your life have you been relating to God through outward performance (on the basis of law), with the accompanying feeling of obligation, guilt, and fear of punishment for not doing it right? How has that affected your life?

147

GOD'S USE OF DISCIPLINE

Read the Truth

Brothers and sisters, if someone is caught in a sin, you who live by the Spirit should restore that person gently. But watch yourselves, or you also may be tempted. (Galatians 6:1)

And the Lord's servant must not be quarrelsome but must be kind to everyone, able to teach, not resentful. Opponents must be gently instructed, in the hope that God will grant them repentance leading them to a knowledge of the truth... (2 Timothy 2:24-25)

All Scripture is God-breathed and is useful for teaching, rebuking, correcting and training in righteousness... (2 Timothy 3:16)

Confirm the Truth

According to Galatians 6:1, what or who does God use to discipline His children?

From 2 Timothy 2:24-25, what or who does God use to discipline His children?

Based on 2 Timothy 3:16, what does God use to discipline His children?

Understand the Truth

Under grace, believers are disciplined in specific ways and for a purpose. Galatians 6:1 tells us that godly individuals are called to restore straying Christians back to the right way of living. Those serving God are given direction by God to instruct everyone according to the Scriptures what is right and what is not right regarding how to live in Christ. The Scriptures themselves are able to teach, rebuke, correct and train every man and woman in the way of righteousness. God uses His own Word plus teachers, mentors, and coaches to accomplish His purposes.

Reflect and Respond

GOD'S USE OF DISCIPLINE

Read the Truth

And we know that in all things God works for the good of those who love Him, who have been called according to His purpose. For those God foreknew He also predestined to be conformed to the image of His Son, that He might be the firstborn among many brothers and sisters. And those He predestined, He also called; those He called, He also justified; those He justified, He also glorified. (Romans 8:28-30)

...being confident of this, that He who began a good work in you will carry it on to completion until the day of Christ Jesus. (Philippians 1:6)

⁴ In your struggle against sin, you have not yet resisted to the point of shedding your blood. ⁵ And have you completely forgotten this word of encouragement that addresses you as a father addresses his son? It says, "My son, do not make light of the Lord's discipline, and do not lose heart when He rebukes you, ⁶ because the Lord disciplines the one he loves, and He chastens everyone He accepts as His son." (Hebrews 12:4-6)

⁷ Endure hardship as discipline; God is treating you as His children. For what children are not disciplined by their father? ⁸ If you are not disciplined—and everyone undergoes discipline—then you are not legitimate, not true sons and daughters at all. ⁹ Moreover, we have all had human fathers who disciplined us and we respected them for it. How much more should we submit to the Father of spirits and live! ¹⁰ They disciplined us for a little while as they thought best; but God disciplines us for our good, in order that we may share in His holiness. ¹¹ No discipline seems pleasant at the time, but painful. Later on, however, it produces a harvest of righteousness and peace for those who have been trained by it. (Hebrews 12:7-11)

Confirm the Truth

Based on Romans 8:28-30, for what purpose does God discipline His children?

What does God promise in Philippians 1:6 regarding His purpose in our lives?

According to Hebrews 12:4-6, why does God discipline His children?

How are we to view hardship (Hebrews 12:7-11)?

Understand the Truth

Because we live under the grace of God in Jesus Christ, believers can rest in the fact that all of God's purposes for us are *good.* We have a loving Father who teaches, trains, and corrects. Even when evil occurs (because we still live in a fallen world), we can rest confidently in the promise of Romans 8:28: *"And we know that God causes all things to work together for good to those who love God, to those who are called according to His purpose."* His desire is to conform us to the image of Christ so that each believer regardless of behavioral style, ethnic background, or abilities can express the same character of Christ in their lives.

Because God loves us so much, He also plans to complete the good work He began in us when we were "born again." And God disciplines us for our good so that we may share in His holiness. Our God is good all the time to us—even in the tough times, in different ways to each of His children, and by what He allows and doesn't allow into our lives.

Reflect and Respond

Consider the means that God uses to train (discipline) you to trust Him more, to depend upon Him more, and to say "no" to selfishness and "yes" to selflessness.

In what ways are you grateful for those lessons that overflowed from His grace and love towards you even if they hurt?

GRACE AND OBEDIENCE

Part 2: Grace motivates us to obedience out of love and gratitude

So why do some Christians so easily stray away from grace into legalism? Why would someone want to retain the Law or create additional laws for Christians to follow? Often, it is because of the fear of lawlessness. All agree that lawlessness is wrong and is to be opposed. Yet, there is the tendency to think sin can be controlled through lots of rules. We all know how much that does not work! The answer, however, is not that we should keep believers under law. It is teaching and exhorting believers to "live by the Spirit"—the better way.

Read the Truth

You, my brothers and sisters, were called to be free. But do not use your freedom to indulge the flesh; rather, serve one another humbly in love. For the entire Law is fulfilled in keeping this one command: "Love your neighbor as yourself." If you bite and devour each other, watch out or you will be destroyed by each other. So I say, walk by the Spirit, and you will not gratify the desires of the flesh. (Galatians 5:13-16)

But God demonstrates His own love for us in this: While we were still sinners, Christ died for us. (Romans 5:8)

For Christ's love compels us, because we are convinced that one died for all, and therefore all died. And He died for all, that those who live should no longer live for themselves but for Him who died for them and was raised again. (2 Corinthians 5:14-15)

Confirm the Truth

In contrast to living by law, how are Christians exhorted to live with our grace-based freedom (Galatians 5:13-16)?

According to Romans 5:8, what should motivate us to obey God with our lives?

From 2 Corinthians 5:14-15, what should motivate us to obey God with our lives?

Understand the Truth

Christians are exhorted to live by the Spirit and not to gratify the desires of the flesh. It is a choice each one must make and can make. The Spirit is a

151

greater power than our weaker wills. Trusting the Spirit to work in and through us is a much better way than to just follow rules.

Through our adoption as sons and the gift of the Holy Spirit, we have received a status as spiritual *adults*. Adults live on the basis of *mature character* with freedom and responsibility. Knowing and understanding your new status in Christ, based on all that Christ has done for you and what you have in Him, helps to answer the question, "Why should I live a godly life if I'm not under law?"

The answer can simply be GRATITUDE—gratitude for God's great LOVE for you. Romans 5:8 describes how much God loves you and how He demonstrated that love through Christ's death on the cross for you. Christ's love compels you to live for Him because of what He did for you.

> A preacher of the Law comes down on men with threats and punishments; a preacher of divine grace coaxes and urges men by reminding them of the goodness and mercy which God has shown them. For He [God] would have no unwilling workers nor cheerless service; He wants men to be glad and cheerful in the service of God. (Martin Luther, comments on Romans 12)

Reflect and Respond

GRACE AND OBEDIENCE

Read the Truth

"Come to me, all you who are weary and burdened, and I will give you rest. Take my yoke upon you and learn from me, for I am gentle and humble in heart, and you will find rest for your souls. For my yoke is easy and my burden is light." (Matthew 11:28-30)

For the grace of God has appeared that offers salvation to all people. It teaches us to say "No" to ungodliness and worldly passions, and to live self-controlled, upright and godly lives in this present age, while we wait for the blessed hope—the appearing of the glory of our great God and Savior, Jesus Christ, who gave Himself for us to redeem us from all wickedness and to purify for Himself a people that are His very own, eager to do what is good. (Titus 2:11-14)

Confirm the Truth

Based on Matthew 11:28-30, what are the benefits of living by grace rather than by law (burdened)?

From Titus 2:11-14, what does grace teach us so we can reach God's goal of godliness in our lives?

Understand the Truth

To those who were weary and burdened from living by Law, Jesus promised rest and help as people trust in Him. Paul declared in Titus 2 that grace teaches us to say no to ungodliness through the Spirit inside. And grace teaches us to live rightly. As a result, we experience joy doing the good work God wants for us to do while we are also waiting for our Savior's return. Grace motivates us to obedience by love and gratitude for what Christ has done.

> What God wants is for us to **trust** Him and His Word—the Word that tells us that Christ has done it all—and to act on it by approaching 'the throne of grace with confidence, so that we may receive mercy and find grace to help in our time of need' (Hebrews 4:16) ...But if you don't trust that you have been made totally acceptable in God's sight, you will never have the boldness to approach Him. You will linger outside His throne room, trying to find a way to get 'worthy' enough to go in. The end result is that you will avoid going to your only source of help (God) when you need Him the most! (Bob George, *Classic Christianity*, p. 102)

Reflect and Respond

GRACE AND OBEDIENCE

Read the Truth

For it is we who are the circumcision, we who serve God by His Spirit, who boast in Christ Jesus, and who put no confidence in the flesh— though I myself have reasons for such confidence. If someone else thinks they have reasons to put confidence in the flesh, I have more: circumcised on the eighth day, of the people of Israel, of the tribe of Benjamin, a Hebrew of Hebrews; in regard to the Law, a Pharisee; as for zeal, persecuting the church; as for righteousness based on the Law, faultless. But whatever were gains to me I now consider loss for the sake of Christ. (Philippians 3:3-7)

What is more, I consider everything a loss because of the surpassing worth of knowing Christ Jesus my Lord, for whose sake I have lost all things. I consider them garbage, that I may gain Christ, and be found in Him, not having a righteousness of my own that comes from the Law, but that which is through faith in Christ—the righteousness that comes from God on the basis of faith. I want to know Christ—yes, to know the power of His resurrection and participation in His sufferings, becoming like Him in His death... (Philippians 3:8-10)

I thank Christ Jesus our Lord, who has given me strength, that He considered me trustworthy, appointing me to His service. Even though I was once a blasphemer and a persecutor and a violent man, I was shown mercy because I acted in ignorance and unbelief. The grace of our Lord was poured out on me abundantly, along with the faith and love that are in Christ Jesus. Here is a trustworthy saying that deserves full acceptance: Christ Jesus came into the world to save sinners—of whom I am the worst. But for that very reason I was shown mercy so that in me, the worst of sinners, Christ Jesus might display His immense patience as an example for those who would believe in Him and receive eternal life. Now to the King eternal, immortal, invisible, the only God, be honor and glory for ever and ever. Amen. (1 Timothy 1:12-17)

Confirm the Truth

How did Paul consider his early life living by Law compared to living by the grace of God in Philippians 3:3-7?

What was of surpassing worth for him (verses 8-10)?

What did Paul learn about the value of grace in his life (1 Timothy 1:12-17)?

Understand the Truth

Paul understood the plight of those who had been relating to God through outward performance under the Law for years. He had been there! Those who have been freed from the Law (both Jews and non-Jews since Christ) can now have a relationship with God on the basis of His **grace**, as Paul describes about his own life (1 Timothy 1:12-17). **Grace motivates us to obedience by love and gratitude for what Christ has done.**

God wants you to relate to Him on the basis of His grace, so that your motivation to obey Him is based on His love for you, your love for Him, and gratitude for what Christ has done for you. Relax! Thank Him that you have freedom to relate to your God on the basis of His GRACE to you. And enjoy your grace-filled relationship with your God today, tomorrow, and forever!

Reflect and Respond

Paul responded to God's grace call on his life with a statement of praise in 1 Timothy 1:17. How will you respond? Feel free to use any creative means including drawing a diagram of your freedom in Christ now.

155

part 8

GRACE-CENTERED LIVING

*I have been crucified with Christ and I no
longer live, but Christ lives in me. The life I live
in the body, I live by faith in the Son of God,
who loved me and gave Himself for me.
(Galatians 2:20)*

HOW ARE CHRISTIANS MEANT TO LIVE?

God does not want believers to live by law but by the Holy Spirit. Whether someone is living by law (God's Law or human-made laws) or by grace is determined by two key issues:

1. The issue of **motivation:** Why you do what you do.
   - Under law, a person works in order to earn or maintain the acceptance of God.
   - Under grace, a person *trusts in Jesus Christ as her acceptance from God* and does good works out of love and gratitude.
2. The issue of **power**: How you do what you do.
   - Under law, a person lives from *her own* power and resources.
   - Under grace, a person lives by *Christ's life and power* imparted by the Holy Spirit.

Read the Truth

But if you are led by the Spirit, you are not under law. (Galatians 5:18)

Now the Lord is the Spirit, and where the Spirit of the Lord is, there is freedom. (2 Corinthians 3:17)

5 For when we were controlled by the sinful nature, the sinful passions aroused by the law were at work in our bodies, so that we bore fruit for death. 6 But now, by dying to what once bound us, we have been released from the law so that we serve in the new way of the Spirit, and not in the old way of the written code. (Romans 7:5-6)

Confirm the Truth

What does Galatians 5:18 declare to you?

Where the Spirit of the Lord is, what is present (2 Corinthians 3:17)?

What is aroused by the way of law (Romans 7:5)?

Why have we been released from the Law (Romans 7:6)?

Understand the Truth

In the New Testament, living by the Holy Spirit is consistently presented in contrast to living by law. When anyone chooses to live by the Spirit, she is at that time not living by the law. The two ways of living are mutually exclusive. Paul writes in 2 Corinthians that where the Spirit of the Lord is, there is freedom. The law never provides freedom. In Romans, we read that the Law once aroused sinful passions leading to death. But Christians are freed from the law to serve in the new way of the Spirit.

Living by the Spirit is a new way of living for any human being. Before Christ, we don't have that option. We live according to our sinful nature. After trusting in Christ, we are freed to choose a new way of living—Spirit-led life. It's a much better way!

Reflect and Respond

DAY 100

THE HOLY SPIRIT IN THE OLD TESTAMENT

>❀➤➤❀➤➤❀➤❀➤❀➤❀❀

Read the Truth

Because of your great compassion you did not abandon them in the wilderness. By day the pillar of cloud did not fail to guide them on their path, nor the pillar of fire by night to shine on the way they were to take. You gave your good Spirit to instruct them. You did not withhold your manna from their mouths, and you gave them water for their thirst. (Nehemiah 9:19-20)

For many years you were patient with them. By your Spirit you warned them through your prophets. Yet they paid no attention, so you gave them into the hands of the neighboring peoples. (Nehemiah 9:30)

Then Moses said to the Israelites, "See, the Lord has chosen Bezalel son of Uri, the son of Hur, of the tribe of Judah, and He has filled him with the Spirit of God, with wisdom, with understanding, with knowledge and with all kinds of skills—to make artistic designs for work in gold, silver and bronze, to cut and set stones, to work in wood and to engage in all kinds of artistic crafts. And He has given both him and Oholiab son of Ahisamak, of the tribe of Dan, the ability to teach others. He has filled them with skill to do all kinds of work as engravers, designers, embroiderers in blue, purple and scarlet yarn and fine linen, and weavers—all of them skilled workers and designers. So Bezalel, Oholiab and every skilled person to whom the Lord has given skill and ability to know how to carry out all the work of constructing the sanctuary are to do the work just as the Lord has commanded." (Exodus 35:30-36:1)

Then Samuel took a flask of olive oil and poured it on Saul's head and kissed him, saying, "Has not the Lord anointed you ruler over his inheritance?...The Spirit of the Lord will come powerfully upon you, and you will prophesy with them; and you will be changed into a different person. Once these signs are fulfilled, do whatever your hand finds to do, for God is with you. Go down ahead of me to Gilgal. I will surely come down to you to sacrifice burnt offerings and fellowship offerings, but you must wait seven days until I come to you and tell you what you are to do." As Saul turned to leave Samuel, God changed Saul's heart, and all these signs were fulfilled that day. (1 Samuel 10:1,6-9)

So he sent for him and had him brought in. He was glowing with health and had a fine appearance and handsome features. Then the Lord said, "Rise and anoint him; this is the one." So Samuel took the horn of oil and anointed him in the presence of his brothers, and from that day on the Spirit of the Lord came powerfully upon David. Samuel then went to Ramah. (1 Samuel 16:12-13)

Confirm the Truth

According to Nehemiah 9:19-20, what was the Spirit's role?

What also was the Spirit's role (Nehemiah 9:30)?

160

From Exodus 35:30-36:1, what did the Holy Spirit enable Bezalel to do?

Based on 1 Samuel 10:6-9, what would the Holy Spirit do for Saul?

According to 1 Samuel 16:12-13, what did the Holy Spirit do to David?

Understand the Truth

Who is the Holy Spirit? The Holy Spirit is *God Himself*, the Third Person of what is called "the Trinity," a designation that also includes God the Father and God the Son (Jesus). The Holy Spirit is described as possessing all the divine attributes and is referred to as God. It is important to remember that the Holy Spirit is a *Person*, not a "force" or merely an impersonal attribute or influence of God. He is described as having all the elements of personality: **intellect** (1 Corinthians 2:11), **emotions** (Ephesians 4:30), and **will** (1 Corinthians 12:11). Personal pronouns are used of Him, such as "He" or "Him" (John 16:7-8). He is God.

The Holy Spirit was active throughout history from creation until the New Testament age. Nehemiah recounts the role of the Spirit in the life of Israel as a nation. In his prayer for Israel, Nehemiah reminded the people that the Spirit was given to instruct them and to warn them of wrongdoing through the prophets. In the desert during the Exodus, the Holy Spirit gifted Bezalel for artistry of all kinds to build the Tabernacle. And that giftedness extended to giving skill to all the craftsmen as well who worked on the Tabernacle. The Holy Spirit came upon Saul when he was made king over Israel by God. The Spirit changed Saul's heart, making him a changed person who was empowered to be king. Later, the Spirit came upon David to give him power to be king of Israel. Whenever the Spirit came upon someone, His presence was evident.

Reflect and Respond

THE PROMISE OF THE HOLY SPIRIT FOR EVERYONE

Read the Truth

And afterward, I will pour out my Spirit on all people. Your sons and daughters will prophesy, your old men will dream dreams, your young men will see visions. Even on my servants, both men and women, I will pour out my Spirit in those days. I will show wonders in the heavens and on the earth, blood and fire and billows of smoke. (Joel 2:28-30)

For I will take you out of the nations; I will gather you from all the countries and bring you back into your own land. I will sprinkle clean water on you, and you will be clean; I will cleanse you from all your impurities and from all your idols. I will give you a new heart and put a new spirit in you; I will remove from you your heart of stone and give you a heart of flesh. And I will put my Spirit in you and move you to follow my decrees and be careful to keep my laws. Then you will live in the land I gave your ancestors; you will be my people, and I will be your God. (Ezekiel 36:24-28)

And so John the Baptist appeared in the wilderness, preaching a baptism of repentance for the forgiveness of sins. The whole Judean countryside and all the people of Jerusalem went out to him. Confessing their sins, they were baptized by him in the Jordan River. John wore clothing made of camel's hair, with a leather belt around his waist, and he ate locusts and wild honey. And this was his message: "After me comes the one more powerful than I, the straps of whose sandals I am not worthy to stoop down and untie. I baptize you with water, but He will baptize you with the Holy Spirit." (Mark 1:4-8)

Confirm the Truth

What did God promise about His Spirit in Joel 2:28-30?

What did God promise about His Spirit in Ezekiel 36:24-28?

Referring to Jesus, what announcement did John the Baptist make about the Spirit (Mark 1:4-8)?

Understand the Truth

The anointing of the Holy Spirit on Old Testament believers was not promised to all believers of that time nor promised to be permanent when given. However, the prophets spoke of a future day, the time of the New Covenant or Kingdom.

162

Joel declared that God's Spirit would be poured out on all people—young and old, men and women, those of any age or stage of life. And the presence of the Spirit in those lives would be evident. God would be praised through the words and work of those receiving the Spirit. Through Ezekiel, God promised that He would put His Spirit into the hearts of people to move them from within to obey Him.

When John the Baptist came on the scene several hundred years later, just before Jesus' ministry began, John declared that he would baptize people with water as a sign of their repentance from sin. But someone was coming after him who would baptize people with the Holy Spirit, thus identifying who were the people of God in whose hearts God would now dwell forever. This would be associated with God establishing His Kingdom on the earth. The time had come. God was ready to do what He had promised to do.

Reflect and Respond

DAY 102

THE COMING OF THE SPIRIT

Read the Truth

Jesus answered, "Very truly I tell you, no one can enter the kingdom of God unless they are born of water and the Spirit. Flesh gives birth to flesh, but the Spirit gives birth to spirit. You should not be surprised at my saying, 'You must be born again.' The wind blows wherever it pleases. You hear its sound, but you cannot tell where it comes from or where it is going. So it is with everyone born of the Spirit." (John 3:5-8)

On the last and greatest day of the festival, Jesus stood and said in a loud voice, "Let anyone who is thirsty come to me and drink. Whoever believes in me, as Scripture has said, rivers of living water will flow from within them." By this He meant the Spirit, whom those who believed in Him were later to receive. Up to that time the Spirit had not been given, since Jesus had not yet been glorified. (John 7:37-39)

After His suffering, He presented Himself to them and gave many convincing proofs that He was alive. He appeared to them over a period of forty days and spoke about the kingdom of God. On one occasion, while He was eating with them, He gave them this command: "Do not leave Jerusalem, but wait for the gift my Father promised, which you have heard me speak about. For John baptized with water, but in a few days you will be baptized with the Holy Spirit." Then they gathered around Him and asked him, "Lord, are you at this time going to restore the kingdom to Israel?" He said to them: "It is not for you to know the times or dates the Father has set by His own authority. But you will receive power when the Holy Spirit comes on you; and you will be my witnesses in Jerusalem, and in all Judea and Samaria, and to the ends of the earth." (Acts 1:3-8)

When the day of Pentecost came, they were all together in one place. Suddenly a sound like the blowing of a violent wind came from heaven and filled the whole house where they were sitting. They saw what seemed to be tongues of fire that separated and came to rest on each of them. All of them were filled with the Holy Spirit and began to speak in other tongues as the Spirit enabled them. (Acts 2:1-4)

No, this is what was spoken by the prophet Joel: "'In the last days, God says, I will pour out my Spirit on all people. (Acts 2:16-17)

Confirm the Truth

What did Jesus say about the Spirit in John 3:5-8?

What did Jesus promise to those who believe in Him in John 7:37-39?

What did Jesus promise to His followers about the Spirit in Acts 1:3-8?

164

Understand the Truth

Jesus promised that the Holy Spirit would cause us to be born again. It was truly a mystery, but those who studied the Scriptures should know this is coming. The Spirit would seem like streams of living water flowing from within. Living water often referred to water from a spring or flowing river. It was fresh, not stagnant, and highly valued. The phrase "living water" also came to be associated with spiritual life. It was an unending supply of vitality and joy. Just before Jesus ascended into Heaven, He told His disciples to stay in Jerusalem and wait for the giving of the Holy Spirit. They would be baptized with the Spirit who would give them power to become Jesus' witnesses everywhere they would go. The prophecy of Joel was fulfilled.

All of those promises from the Old Testament and from Jesus' own teaching were fulfilled on the day of Pentecost (50 days after the crucifixion). Many of Jesus' followers were gathered together praying. God responded by filling them with His Spirit in a very dramatic, recognizable, and unforgettable way. A new time had come. Peter preached a powerful sermon, urging the listeners to believe that Jesus was Christ the Lord.

Those who accepted his message were baptized, and about three thousand were added to their number that day. (Acts 2:41

Does the concept of the Holy Spirit's existence seem like science fiction to you? Like something out of a movie, e.g. "the force is with you" from *Star Wars*? We often feel this way because His name is more like a title. We have God the Father (we can relate to "father") and God the Son (whose name is Jesus, we can relate to "son" and "Jesus"). Paul often refers to the Spirit as the Spirit of Christ or God's Spirit to help us relate to Him. Be honest with God here. Let Him know how you feel. Ask Him to help you trust what He says in His Word about HIs Spirit's presence in our world and in our lives.

Reflect and Respond

165

THE RELATIONAL MINISTRY OF THE HOLY SPIRIT

When a person hears the Gospel and places her faith in Jesus Christ, several things happen instantaneously as a one-time event regarding the work of the Holy Spirit. These are a review and confirmation of what you have already learned about your identity in Christ.

Read the Truth

But when the kindness and love of God our Savior appeared, He saved us, not because of righteous things we had done, but because of His mercy. He saved us through the washing of rebirth and renewal by the Holy Spirit, whom He poured out on us generously through Jesus Christ our Savior... (Titus 3:4-6)

You, however, are not in the realm of the flesh but are in the realm of the Spirit, if indeed the Spirit of God lives in you. And if anyone does not have the Spirit of Christ, they do not belong to Christ. (Romans 8:9

The Spirit Himself testifies with our spirit that we are God's children. (Romans 8:16

Confirm the Truth

At the moment of salvation (when one believes), what is done by the Holy Spirit (Titus 3:4-6)?

What are the benefits of being in the realm of the Spirit (Romans 8:9)?

What does the Spirit reveal to us as believers (Romans 8:16?

Understand the Truth

At the moment of salvation, the Holy Spirit enacts rebirth and renewal to every new believer. In other words, you were born again and given life (regeneration). Don't you love how Paul described this gift of the Spirit as "whom He poured out on us generously through Jesus Christ our Savior?" *Generously* is a purposeful word.

Our generous God gives His Spirit to live inside each believer and identify her as belonging to Christ. This is a declaration about our status with God and a promise of lasting relationship. *Belonging* reaches to our core need for love and security. Those without the Spirit do not belong to Christ. What a sad conclusion!

The Spirit also reveals to believers that they are now God's children. This is a ministry of the Spirit to us, enabling a new relationship with God as our Father, a loving Father. Maybe you haven't had such a great earthly father, but you have imagined what having a loving Father who delights in you as His child would be like. Your Father God is better than the best earthly father that you could ever imagine. You are the child of the living God. Woohoo!

Reflect and Respond

THE RELATIONAL MINISTRY OF THE HOLY SPIRIT

Read the Truth

But when the set time had fully come, God sent His Son, born of a woman, born under the law, to redeem those under the law, that we might receive adoption to sonship. Because you are His sons, God sent the Spirit of His Son into our hearts, the Spirit who calls out, "Abba, Father." So you are no longer a slave, but God's child; and since you are His child, God has made you also an heir. (Galatians 4:4-7)

For we were all baptized by one Spirit so as to form one body—whether Jews or Gentiles, slave or free—and we were all given the one Spirit to drink. (1 Corinthians 12:13)

And you also were included in Christ when you heard the message of truth, the gospel of your salvation. When you believed, you were marked in Him with a seal, the promised Holy Spirit, who is a deposit guaranteeing our inheritance until the redemption of those who are God's possession—to the praise of His glory. (Ephesians 1:13-14)

Confirm the Truth

According to Galatians 4:4-7, what does the Spirit of God do for us?

Based on 1 Corinthians 12:13, what does the Spirit of God do for us?

From Ephesians 1:13-14, what does the Spirit of God do for us?

Understand the Truth

God sent His Spirit into our hearts, teaching us to call out to God as our "Abba," which is more like the familiar "Daddy" or "Papa" rather than the formal "Father." We can talk to our God on the basis of our relationship with Him as His child, someone who is dearly loved.

When we are individually baptized with the Spirit at the moment of our salvation, we are also baptized into the Body of Christ. Every believer who existed from the day the Spirit was given at Pentecost through the present time is a member of the Body of Christ, also known as the Church (capital "C"). We all share the same Spirit and the same relationship with both Christ as our Lord and God as our Father. This enhances our relationship with each other in the Body of Christ as well.

The Holy Spirit also places God's seal of ownership on us. The seal in Roman times represented the one in authority. Whatever seal the Spirit uses, God recognizes that as belonging to Him. And He will fulfill all the promises He made to those who believe in His Son. The Spirit is a guarantee that when we die, we will be saved from God's judgment and given a place in God's Heaven to dwell forever with God.

All of these wonderful things are part of the Holy Spirit's relational ministry to us. The Spirit does these for us instantaneously at the moment we place our faith in Jesus Christ. We do nothing. God does everything. We get to enjoy the relational benefits.

Reflect and Respond

THE RELATIONAL MINISTRY OF THE HOLY SPIRIT

Read the Truth

"If you love me, keep my commands. And I will ask the Father, and He will give you another advocate to help you and be with you forever—the Spirit of truth. The world cannot accept Him, because it neither sees Him nor knows Him. But you know Him, for He lives with you and will be in you. I will not leave you as orphans; I will come to you. Before long, the world will not see me anymore, but you will see me. Because I live, you also will live. On that day you will realize that I am in my Father, and you are in me, and I am in you." (John 14:15-20)

"But the Advocate, the Holy Spirit, whom the Father will send in my name, will teach you all things and will remind you of everything I have said to you" (John 14:26)

"I have much more to say to you, more than you can now bear. But when He, the Spirit of truth, comes, He will guide you into all the truth. He will not speak on His own; He will speak only what He hears, and He will tell you what is yet to come. He will glorify me because it is from me that He will receive what He will make known to you. All that belongs to the Father is mine. That is why I said the Spirit will receive from me what He will make known to you." (John 16:12-15)

Confirm the Truth

What is the Spirit's role for believers according to John 14:15-20?

What is the Spirit's role for believers according to John 14:26?

What is the Spirit's role for believers according to John 16:12-15?

Understand the Truth

The Holy Spirit will act as an *advocate* for us. The Greek word Jesus used there means to come alongside in order to strengthen or encourage. He is the one who strengthens and encourages us whenever we ask for help. As our encourager, the Spirit will be with us forever! He also connects us to Jesus so that we will never be alone. The Spirit will lead us to obey Jesus' commands in the same way that Jesus obeyed God's commands. He will teach us what Jesus wants us to know. God's Spirit will also guide us into Jesus' truth and to make known to us all that Jesus gives to us. Like Christ, Jesus comes to serve.

170

Through the Holy Spirit, Jesus Christ has established with believers a relationship with Himself similar to the one He enjoyed with the Father. Jesus said, "Don't you believe that I am in the Father, and that the Father is in Me?" (John 14:10). He then said that when the Holy Spirit comes, "On that day you will realize that I am in My Father, and **you are in Me, and I am in you**" (John 14:20). Authentic Christian living is when we live in the same relation to Jesus as He did with His father (love, dependence, and obedience). We trust; He supplies the life and power!

Your position *in Christ* is your:

- Acceptance before God.
- Assurance of salvation.
- Identity.

Christ's presence *in you* is:

- Life (regeneration).
- Power for living.
- The basis of a relationship.
- Promise and hope – the Holy Spirit is called a "deposit" or "down payment" on our salvation, giving assurance of the completion of His work. (Ephesians 1:13-14)

Reflect and Respond

THE EMPOWERING MINISTRY OF THE HOLY SPIRIT

Read the Truth

I have been crucified with Christ and I no longer live, but Christ lives in me. The life I now live in the body, I live by faith in the Son of God, who loved me and gave Himself for me. (Galatians 2:20)

...for it is God who works in you to will and to act in order to fulfill His good purpose. (Philippians 2:13)

To this end I strenuously contend with all the energy Christ so powerfully works in me. (Colossians 1:29)

Confirm the Truth

According to Galatians 2:20, how is the Christian life to be lived?

Based on Philippians 2:13, who enables you to live the Christian life?

From Colossians 1:29, who enables you to live the Christian life?

Understand the Truth

From the beginning of our faith relationship with Jesus Christ, the Holy Spirit anoints us with God's presence and power. We need both to live the kind of life Jesus intends for us to live. After this one-time work of the Spirit to establish God's presence within us, He has an ongoing empowering ministry in the life of every believer. The genuine Christian life is to be lived by faith in Christ who is living in us. We are to yield our wills to God's work in us as He sees fit to work out His purpose in our lives. The work of Christ's power in us is far more powerful than our own. Our striving should be in sync with His work and purposes in our lives. All of this is enabled through the Holy Spirit's empowering presence in us.

Reflect and Respond

THE EMPOWERING MINISTRY OF THE HOLY SPIRIT

Read the Truth

After they prayed, the place where they were meeting was shaken. And they were all filled with the Holy Spirit and spoke the word of God boldly. (Acts 4:31)

And hope does not put us to shame, because God's love has been poured out into our hearts through the Holy Spirit, who has been given to us. (Romans 5:5)

In the same way, the Spirit helps us in our weakness. We do not know what we ought to pray for, but the Spirit Himself intercedes for us through wordless groans. And He who searches our hearts knows the mind of the Spirit, because the Spirit intercedes for God's people in accordance with the will of God. (Romans 8:26-27)

Confirm the Truth

What does the Holy Spirit's filling empower the believer to do (Acts 4:31)?

What does the Holy Spirit empower the believer to have (Romans 5:5)?

From Romans 8:26-27, what does the Holy Spirit do for the believer?

Understand the Truth

The Holy Spirit is the means by which Christ is "with us" and "in us." Christ is in a glorified human body in Heaven. He is with us by means of the Holy Spirit. To sum up: The ongoing ministry of the Holy Spirit has been well expressed by scholar Gordon D. Fee in the phrase, *"God's Empowering Presence."* That is what He is and does. In His empowering ministry to every believer, He enables us to speak the Word of God boldly (Acts 4:31). From Romans 5, we see that the Spirit enables us to feel God's love for us, and He fills us with hope that God is at work within us and for us according to His promises. One of the most comforting ways the Spirit empowers us is in prayer. When we are weak, He carries our prayer needs directly to God the Father or God the Son and then works in our lives according to what is needed for us. At times of crisis, we can have confidence that God both hears our need and acts upon it on our behalf.

Reflect and Respond

THE EMPOWERING MINISTRY OF THE HOLY SPIRIT

Read the Truth

However, as it is written: "What no eye has seen, what no ear has heard, and what no human mind has conceived"—the things God has prepared for those who love Him—these are the things God has revealed to us by His Spirit. The Spirit searches all things, even the deep things of God. For who knows a person's thoughts except their own spirit within them? In the same way no one knows the thoughts of God except the Spirit of God. What we have received is not the spirit of the world, but the Spirit who is from God, so that we may understand what God has freely given us. (1 Corinthians 2:9-12)

This is what we speak, not in words taught us by human wisdom but in words taught by the Spirit, explaining spiritual realities with Spirit-taught words. The person without the Spirit does not accept the things that come from the Spirit of God but considers them foolishness, and cannot understand them because they are discerned only through the Spirit. The person with the Spirit makes judgments about all things, but such a person is not subject to merely human judgments, for, "Who has known the mind of the Lord so as to instruct Him?" But we have the mind of Christ. (1 Corinthians 2:13-16)

Confirm the Truth

From 1 Corinthians 2:9-12, what does the Holy Spirit empower the believer to do?

From 1 Corinthians 2:13-16, what does the Holy Spirit empower the believer to do?

Understand the Truth

The Holy Spirit reveals to us the things that God has prepared for those who love Him. By His enabling power within our own spirits, we are empowered to understand what God has freely given us. The Spirit explains to us spiritual truth through His access to our minds. It is He who helps us to understand the Word of God when we read and study it. Many concepts in the Bible are foolishness to those without the Spirit. Thanks to the Spirit's empowering ministry, we are able to discern spiritual truth and understand how to apply it to our lives. And the most incredible statement of all is this, "We have the mind of Christ." All of this we receive because of the Holy Spirit's empowering presence in our lives.

Reflect and Respond

THE EMPOWERING MINISTRY OF THE HOLY SPIRIT

Read the Truth

There are different kinds of gifts, but the same Spirit distributes them. There are different kinds of service, but the same Lord. There are different kinds of working, but in all of them and in everyone it is the same God at work. Now to each one the manifestation of the Spirit is given for the common good. To one there is given through the Spirit a message of wisdom, to another a message of knowledge by means of the same Spirit, to another faith by the same Spirit, to another gifts of healing by that one Spirit, to another miraculous powers, to another prophecy, to another distinguishing between spirits, to another speaking in different kinds of tongues, and to still another the interpretation of tongues. All these are the work of one and the same Spirit, and He distributes them to each one, just as He determines. (1 Corinthians 12:4-11)

For this reason I kneel before the Father, from whom every family in heaven and on earth derives its name. I pray that out of His glorious riches He may strengthen you with power through His Spirit in your inner being, so that Christ may dwell in your hearts through faith. And I pray that you, being rooted and established in love, may have power, together with all the Lord's holy people, to grasp how wide and long and high and deep is the love of Christ, and to know this love that surpasses knowledge—that you may be filled to the measure of all the fullness of God. (Ephesians 3:14-19)

Now to Him who is able to do immeasurably more than all we ask or imagine, according to His power that is at work within us, to Him be glory in the Church and in Christ Jesus throughout all generations, for ever and ever! Amen. (Ephesians 3:20-21)

Confirm the Truth

What empowerment of the Holy Spirit is revealed in 1 Corinthians 12:4-11?

What does the Holy Spirit empower the believer to do (Ephesians 3:14-19)?

What is revealed about the Holy Spirit's power in Ephesians 3:20-21?

Understand the Truth

Paul describes the work of the Spirit in 1 Corinthians 12 by the various gifts the Spirit distributes to individual believers by His own choice and will. Through these Spirit-given gifts, believers are empowered to do specific

works of ministry to one another in the whole Body of Christ. In this way also, the Holy Spirit enables believers to work together for the common good of all.

One of the greatest works of the Spirit in all believers is to strengthen us with His power so that we will know how dearly loved we are. Isn't it great to know this unbounded love for us and experience it so wonderfully? If that is not enough, Paul finishes off by saying that the Spirit fills us with the fullness of God. We have God's complete empowering presence in us giving us the kind of life that God wants us to know and experience. The Spirit's power is at work within us. He does more than we can ask or imagine for us with the end result that Jesus Christ gets the praise and glory!

Reflect and Respond

Briefly describe a great need that God has met in your life or a remarkable thing that God has done in your life through His Spirit's empowering presence in you.

WALKING BY THE SPIRIT

Read the Truth

Those who live according to the flesh have their minds set on what the flesh desires; but those who live in accordance with the Spirit have their minds set on what the Spirit desires. (Romans 8:5)

For those who are led by the Spirit of God are the children of God. (Romans 8:14)

So I say, walk by the Spirit, and you will not gratify the desires of the flesh. (Galatians 5:16)

But if you are led by the Spirit, you are not under the law. (Galatians 5:18)

Since we live by the Spirit, let us keep in step with the Spirit. (Galatians 5:25)

Confirm the Truth

What is true about those who live in accordance with the Spirit (Romans 8:5)?

What is true about those who are led by the Spirit (Romans 8:14; Galatians 5:18)?

What will be true for those who walk by or live by the Spirit (Galatians 5:16, 25)?

Understand the Truth

The New Testament encourages believers to "walk by the Spirit" (Galatians 5:16), "live by/in accordance with the Spirit" (Romans 8:5; Galatians 5:25) and be "led by the Spirit" (Romans 8:14; Galatians 5:18). The Greek word Paul used here in Galatians 5:16 means to literally "walk"—a common idiom for how one conducts one's life or how one behaves, in this case one's faith walk. What does it mean to walk by the Spirit?

Walking by the Spirit means walking in submission to and dependence on the Spirit. As Paul wrote in Romans 1:17,

"For in the gospel a righteousness from God is revealed, a righteousness that is by faith from first to last, just as it is written: 'The righteous will live by faith.'"

We exercise faith in Jesus Christ for our salvation. We exercise faith for our daily living out the life of Christ within us. This daily faith walk by the Spirit involves every area of life.

At the beginning of this section, you learned that you can recognize if you are living by law or living by the Spirit based on two areas:

- The issue of motivation: Why you do what you do. Under law, a person works in order to earn the acceptance of God. Under grace, a person trusts in Jesus Christ as her acceptance, and works from love and gratitude. You know you are living by the Spirit when your response to God is to serve Him out of your love for Him and gratitude for what He has done for you.

- The issue of power: How you do what you do. Under law, a person lives from her own power and resources. Under grace, a person lives by Christ's life and power imparted by the Holy Spirit. You know you are living by the Spirit when you are stepping out in obedience to God's Word, depending on God for the ability and power to do what He asks you to do, and trusting God with the results.

Reflect and Respond

Do you recognize areas of your life—relationships, school, work, emotions, health, parenting, finances—where you are relying on your own power rather than the Spirit's power? Consider giving over those areas to your God and begin trusting in the Spirit's power. Choose to live according to the Spirit and be led by the Spirit in those areas. Trust your God with the results and watch what happens!

THE FILLING OF THE SPIRIT

➤➤➤➤➤➤❀❀❀❀❀

The Holy Spirit connects us with Christ so that He is *with us* and *in us* forever—God's presence. The Holy Spirit empowers us to live the kind of life our God asks us to live—God's power. He is God's empowering presence. We are called to live by the Spirit, that is, to walk in submission to and dependence on the Spirit by faith daily.

Read the Truth

Do not get drunk on wine, which leads to debauchery. Instead, be filled with the Spirit, (Ephesians 5:18)

...speaking to one another with psalms, hymns, and songs from the Spirit. Sing and make music from your heart to the Lord, always giving thanks to God the Father for everything, in the name of our Lord Jesus Christ. Submit to one another out of reverence for Christ. (Ephesians 5:19-21)

Confirm the Truth

What instruction does Paul give in Ephesians 5:18?

Why would the comparison to drunkenness be a good one?

Paul referred to four of the many results of the Spirit's filling in Ephesians 5:19-21. What are they?

Understand the Truth

What does it mean to be "filled with the Spirit" (Ephesians 5:18)? The contrast between being filled with wine and filled with the Spirit is obvious. Both forces are internal. When Paul says to "be filled," the words he chose actually mean, "Be being kept filled by the Spirit." Being kept filled amounts to letting the indwelling Holy Spirit control us completely. We do this by trusting and obeying Him as His Word directs. The wine that fills a person controls every area of her life as long as that person consumes it. Drunkenness results in ungodly behavior. Likewise, the believer who allows the Spirit to influence and direct her thinking and behavior will experience Spirit control as long as she yields her will to the Spirit. This is our ongoing responsibility (present tense), and it is expected of every Christian, not optional.

Filling of the Spirit involves our **yielding** to God as God and yielding to His purposes and His truth. God fills what you open. Author Warren Wiersbe says this, "The baptism of the Spirit means that I belong to Christ's body. The filling of the Spirit means that my body belongs to Christ." (Adapted from *Dr. Constable's Notes on Ephesians,* p. 61)

Paul listed several evidences of being filled by the Spirit, including speaking spiritual praises to one another, singing and making music in your heart to the Lord, always giving thanks to God the Father for everything, and submitting to one another out of reverence for Christ. Outwardly, **a filled Christian is expressing joy of the Lord to others. Inwardly, she is expressing joy of the Lord to God Himself.**

All that you have learned so far about evidence of living by the Spirit would apply to evidence of being filled by the Spirit. Both result from yielding to and depending upon the Spirit's empowering presence in your life, choosing God's purposes and truth for your life. Both produce the characteristics of God's life in yours.

Reflect and Respond

THE FILLING OF THE SPIRIT

Read the Truth

12 Therefore, as God's chosen people, holy and dearly loved, clothe yourselves with compassion, kindness, humility, gentleness and patience.13 Bear with each other and forgive one another if any of you has a grievance against someone. Forgive as the Lord forgave you. 14 And over all these virtues put on love, which binds them all together in perfect unity. (Colossians 3:12-14)

15 Let the peace of Christ rule in your hearts, since as members of one body you were called to peace. And be thankful. 16 Let the message of Christ dwell among you richly as you teach and admonish one another with all wisdom through psalms, hymns, and songs from the Spirit, singing to God with gratitude in your hearts. 17 And whatever you do, whether in word or deed, do it all in the name of the Lord Jesus, giving thanks to God the Father through Him. (Colossians 3:15-17)

But the fruit of the Spirit is love, joy, peace, forbearance, kindness, goodness, faithfulness, gentleness and self-control. Against such things there is no law. (Galatians 5:22-23)

Confirm the Truth

What Paul wrote in Colossians 3:12-17 describes more evidence of the Spirit's filling. What are the evidences of being filled with the Spirit/living by the Spirit in each of the following verses?

Verse 12—

Verse 13—

Verse 14—

Verse 15—

Verse 16—

Verse 17—

In Galatians 5:22-23, what are similar evidences of living by the Spirit/being filled by the Spirit, which Paul calls "fruit of the Spirit?"

Understand the Truth

The wonderful evidences of being filled by the Spirit are seemingly endless. When we are living by the Spirit, our lives will be characterized by love, joy, peace, compassion, kindness, humility, gentleness, and patience. We will bear with each other and forgive whatever grievances we have against each other just as God forgives us in Christ. We will let the peace of Christ rule in our hearts and the word of Christ dwell in us richly as we teach and admonish others with all wisdom. We will sing psalms, hymns, and spiritual songs. And we will do and say everything in the name of the Lord Jesus. All this will be done with lots of gratitude. Our lives will be characterized by gratefulness in everything. Can you imagine what kind of life we would enjoy if we lived this way, filled by the Spirit?

> When he [Paul] speaks [in Ephesians 5:18] of being with the Spirit and when he speaks in Colossians of being under the rule of the peace of Christ and indwelt by the "word of Christ," he means to be under God's control. The effect of this control is essentially the same in both passages: a happy, mutual encouragement to praise God and a healthy, mutual relationship with people. (*NIV Study Bible,* note on Ephesians 5:18, p. 1798)

We are not able to produce this beautifully described Christian life on our own. Only Christ can produce it in us as we live dependently on Him.

> We are to maintain a dependent, receiving attitude—the same attitude of availability that Jesus presented to His Father for 33 years. And Christ will produce the fruit of His life in us. Our response should be, "Lord, I can't, but you can." (Bob George, *Classic Christianity*, p. 177)

Human parents raise their children to become more independent of them over time. God raises His children to become more dependent on Him over time. Living by the Spirit / being filled by the Spirit is dependent living.

"The righteous will live by faith" (Romans 1:17). Living by faith is acting according to the Word of God, depending on Jesus Christ for the power, and trusting Him with the results.

Reflect and Respond

From the evidences of living by the Spirit you discovered in the verses above, choose a few that you desire in your life. Now, ask Jesus Christ to produce these in you by saying for each one, "Lord Jesus, I can't, but you can. I want you to do this in my life. I trust you to do this in my life." Watch what He does!

THE HOLY SPIRIT'S UNSEEN PRESENCE

We cannot see the Holy Spirit inside of us. But we know He is working because we become aware of the evidence. These are some things the Spirit does for you:

He helps you understand what the Bible teaches. Has someone explained something to you about the Bible, and you understood what was being said? That's the Spirit inside of you helping you to understand. *John 16:13; 1 Cor. 2:13*

He gives you the words to tell others about Jesus and say that Jesus is God. Have you wanted to tell someone about Jesus but didn't know what to say, then all of a sudden, the words just popped into your head for you to tell that person about Jesus? That's the Holy Spirit living inside of you prompting you with the right words to say. *John 14:26; 1 Corinthians 12:3*

He gives you assurance that you are God's children. Have you ever felt really loved by God? That's the Spirit inside of you letting you know for sure that you are God's child, and He loves you. *Romans 8:16*

He makes you want to do what pleases God. Do you have a desire to please God with your life? That's the Holy Spirit inside of you giving you that desire. *Romans 12:11; Jer. 33:31,33*

He helps you to feel joy as you serve Jesus and when you do the right things. Have you ever felt really good when you chose to do the right thing or chose serve others? That's the Holy Spirit inside of you letting you feel God's pleasure. *Romans 14:17-18*

He makes you not want to do what doesn't please God. Have you ever felt something tugging at you inside when you were tempted to do something wrong? That's the Holy Spirit living inside of you nudging you, reminding you what doesn't please God so you can choose not to do that. We can ask Him to let us know in our thinking or feelings when we are tempted to do something bad. He promises to do that. *Galatians 5:16*

He makes you to become more like Jesus, especially in loving other people. Have you ever started loving someone even more after you started praying for him or her? That's the Holy Spirit living inside of you doing that. *Galatians 5:22-23*

He makes you want to sing praises to God, in your heart and out loud, and be thankful for God's goodness. Do you like to sing praises to God? Do you feel thankful to God for His goodness to you? That's the Spirit living inside of you filling your heart with praise and thanksgiving to God. *Ephesians 5:18-20*

He prays for you when you need help or don't know how to pray. Have you ever had a huge problem and didn't know what to ask God to do about it, but God took care of the problem anyway? That's the Holy Spirit living inside of you working to take care of your need before you even ask. *Romans 8:26-27*

Reflect and Respond

Which of the evidences you just read have you recognized in your life? Thank God for specific ways and times His Spirit has worked in your life.

part 9

GRACE-MOTIVATED OBEDIENCE

*For the grace of God that brings salvation has appeared to all men. **It [grace] teaches us to say 'No' to ungodliness and worldly passions**, and to live self-controlled, upright and godly lives in this present age, while we wait for the blessed hope — the glorious appearing of our great God and Savior, Jesus Christ, who gave himself for us to redeem us from all wickedness and to purify for himself a people that are his very own, eager to do what is good. (Titus 2:11-14)*

GRACE-MOTIVATED OBEDIENCE

Read the Truth

For the grace of God has appeared that offers salvation to all people. It teaches us to say "No" to ungodliness and worldly passions, and to live self-controlled, upright and godly lives in this present age, while we wait for the blessed hope—the appearing of the glory of our great God and Savior, Jesus Christ, who gave Himself for us to redeem us from all wickedness and to purify for Himself a people that are His very own, eager to do what is good. (Titus 2:11-14)

I am the vine; you are the branches. If you remain in me and I in you, you will bear much fruit; apart from me you can do nothing. (John 15:5)

Confirm the Truth

According to Titus 2:11-14, where do we learn obedience?

What did Jesus say about our ability to bear fruit apart from Him (John 15:5)?

Understand the Truth

God's grace will teach us to say no to ungodly behavior and thoughts and to choose the ways to live godly lives in our daily existence. We cannot obey God apart from Jesus Christ and His Spirit living inside of us. In fact, in John 15, Jesus told His disciples that they could do nothing fruitful that pleases God, apart from staying connected to Jesus. Every day. All the time. That's the biblical view of Christian living while we are waiting for Jesus to return.

LIFE IN THE UNTIL TIME

Any attempt to present a realistic and biblical view of Christian living must take into account where we fit in God's plan of history. We live in an overlapping age—possessing the life of the new creation to come through the Holy Spirit, while still living in bodies of the old, fallen creation in a fallen, evil world. That puts us in an ***already but not yet*** tension. We are already justified in God's eyes, but we are not yet made sinless because we still commit sins. We are citizens of the kingdom, but the kingdom has not yet come to earth. Therefore, we need to understand Christian living in a way that **neither underestimates nor overestimates** the quality of life available to us in Jesus Christ.

Those who **underestimate** the quality of life and power available to us through Jesus Christ and the giving of the Spirit will tend to approach Christian living legalistically with **self-confidence**. They believe they can accumulate Christian character through self-disciplined obedience (living by law). In other words, these believers revert to law in an attempt to perfect themselves.

186

Those who **overestimate** the quality of life and power available through the Holy Spirit will tend to approach Christian living mystically (rather than rationally) with **self-confidence**. They believe that their possession of the "fullness of the Spirit" has lifted them beyond the power of sin in the flesh and beyond the power of evil present in the world. These believe that success, prosperity and health belong to people of faith. Suffering, failure, and illness result from a lack of faith.

Both lead to what is called a "triumphalist" approach to spiritual growth, characterized by **confidence in self** and a dangerously low level of respect for one's sinful potential. Triumphalism is revealed by:

- A low-level of perceived need for Christ. His words, "apart from me you can do **nothing**" (John 15:5), have little meaning.
- The common response to our own failures or to the failures of other believers, "I can't believe I/he/she did that!" Shock that we still sin.

Added to the above wrong assumptions about the Christian life is the belief that the flesh improves and becomes "godly" over time, becoming less able to be tempted in the process and becoming less dependent on Christ. Christians who believe this are prime targets for failure, because they tend to play with fire and let down their guard against temptation.

This is the truth: **We *never* outgrow our need to depend 100% upon Jesus Christ.** Spiritual maturity is not reached by needing less of Jesus but by depending more on His truth and His power to live a life that brings glory to God and pleases Him.

Reflect and Respond

THE CONFLICT BETWEEN THE SPIRIT AND THE FLESH

Read the Truth

We know that the law is spiritual; but I am unspiritual, sold as a slave to sin. I do not understand what I do. For what I want to do I do not do, but what I hate I do. And if I do what I do not want to do, I agree that the law is good. As it is, it is no longer I myself who do it, but it is sin living in me. For I know that good itself does not dwell in me, that is, in my sinful nature. For I have the desire to do what is good, but I cannot carry it out. For I do not do the good I want to do, but the evil I do not want to do—this I keep on doing. Now if I do what I do not want to do, it is no longer I who do it, but it is sin living in me that does it. So I find this law at work: Although I want to do good, evil is right there with me. For in my inner being I delight in God's law; but I see another law at work in me, waging war against the law of my mind and making me a prisoner of the law of sin at work within me. What a wretched man I am! Who will rescue me from this body that is subject to death? (Romans 7:14-24)

Confirm the truth

What does Paul write in Romans 7:14-24 describing the experience of people who are trying to be good (on their own) yet are hampered by the flesh?

Understand the Truth

What Paul writes in Romans 7:14-24 describes the universal experience of people who are trying to be good (on their own) yet are hampered by the flesh. The context is applicable to believers and unbelievers alike. Paul's words describe what happens when your mind wants to do what God wants, but your flesh refuses to cooperate. "That which I would not, that do I do." While we as redeemed and justified believers have new life in Christ, we retain our old bodies in which sin dwells (the flesh or sinful nature). This is described as the conflict between the Spirit and the flesh.

What is the flesh? The term "flesh" (NIV: "sinful nature") refers to the *unredeemed* portion of our humanity—our bodies and souls through which indwelling sin assaults us. We don't know what it is, but we know how it works—sending messages to the mind that are in conflict with the Spirit. The flesh does not improve or change its nature over time, as long as we are in our bodies! At the moment of salvation, we are born again of the Spirit. Our bodies are **not** born again, and our souls (mind, emotions, and will) are **not** instantly transformed. While the flesh doesn't improve, our choices can change over time as we learn to live by the Spirit (what you learned in the last section).

Reflect and Respond

THE CONFLICT BETWEEN THE SPIRIT AND THE FLESH

Read the Truth

What causes fights and quarrels among you? Don't they come from your desires that battle within you? (James 4:1)

Dear friends, I urge you, as foreigners and exiles, to abstain from sinful desires, which wage war against your soul. (1 Peter 2:11)

So I say, walk by the Spirit, and you will not gratify the desires of the flesh. For the flesh desires what is contrary to the Spirit, and the Spirit what is contrary to the flesh. They are in conflict with each other, so that you are not to do whatever you want. But if you are led by the Spirit, you are not under the law. (Galatians 5:16-18)

Confirm the Truth

What does James 4:1 say about our struggle with the flesh?

What does 1 Peter 2:11 say about our struggle with the flesh?

What does Galatians 5:16-18 add to our understanding about this conflict?

Understand the Truth

James described the inner struggle as "desires that battle within you." Peter said our sinful desires "wage war" against the Spirit in our souls. Paul confirmed this when he wrote that the flesh desires what is contrary to the Spirit and vice versa. They are in conflict with each other. Battle. War. Sounds serious, doesn't it?

> To live 'according to the flesh' is to live in keeping with the values and desires of life in the present age that stand in absolute contradiction to God and His ways... here designated as opposition to [living by] the Spirit. (Gordon D. Fee, *God's Empowering Presence: The Holy Spirit in the Letters of Paul*)

This opposition is with us every day. We must make a choice every day whether to give into living by the flesh or choose to live by the Spirit.

Reflect and Respond

THE CONFLICT BETWEEN THE SPIRIT AND THE FLESH

Read the Truth

The acts of the flesh are obvious: sexual immorality, impurity and debauchery; idolatry and witchcraft; hatred, discord, jealousy, fits of rage, selfish ambition, dissensions, factions and envy; drunkenness, orgies, and the like. I warn you, as I did before, that those who live like this will not inherit the kingdom of God. But the fruit of the Spirit is love, joy, peace, forbearance, kindness, goodness, faithfulness, gentleness and self-control. Against such things there is no law. Those who belong to Christ Jesus have crucified the flesh with its passions and desires. Since we live by the Spirit, let us keep in step with the Spirit. Let us not become conceited, provoking and envying each other. (Galatians 5:19-26)

Confirm the Truth

From Galatians 5:19-26, what is the evidence of living by the flesh?

From Galatians 5:19-26, what is the evidence of living by the Spirit?

Understand the Truth

The acts of the flesh are sexual immorality, impurity and debauchery; idolatry and witchcraft; hatred, discord, jealousy, fits of rage, selfish ambition, dissensions, factions and envy; drunkenness, orgies, and the like. Paul added becoming conceited, provoking and envying each other to that list. Not a pretty picture!

Living by the Spirit produces godly behavior that includes love, joy, peace, forbearance, kindness, goodness, faithfulness, gentleness and self-control. A much better-looking life, wouldn't you say?

Reflect and Respond

THE CONFLICT BETWEEN THE SPIRIT AND THE FLESH

Read the Truth

Therefore each of you must put off falsehood and speak truthfully to your neighbor, for we are all members of one body. "In your anger do not sin": Do not let the sun go down while you are still angry, and do not give the devil a foothold. Anyone who has been stealing must steal no longer, but must work, doing something useful with their own hands, that they may have something to share with those in need. Do not let any unwholesome talk come out of your mouths, but only what is helpful for building others up according to their needs, that it may benefit those who listen. And do not grieve the Holy Spirit of God, with whom you were sealed for the day of redemption. Get rid of all bitterness, rage and anger, brawling and slander, along with every form of malice. Be kind and compassionate to one another, forgiving each other, just as in Christ God forgave you. (Ephesians 4:25-32)

Follow God's example, therefore, as dearly loved children and walk in the way of love, just as Christ loved us and gave Himself up for us as a fragrant offering and sacrifice to God. But among you there must not be even a hint of sexual immorality, or of any kind of impurity, or of greed, because these are improper for God's holy people. Nor should there be obscenity, foolish talk or coarse joking, which are out of place, but rather thanksgiving...For you were once darkness, but now you are light in the Lord. Live as children of light (for the fruit of the light consists in all goodness, righteousness and truth) and find out what pleases the Lord. (Ephesians 5:1-4, 8-10)

Confirm the Truth

From Ephesians 4:25-32, what is the evidence of living by the flesh?

From Ephesians 4:25-32, what is the evidence of living by the Spirit?

From Ephesians 5:1-4, 8-10, what is the evidence of living by the flesh?

From Ephesians 5:1-4, 8-10, what is the evidence of living by the Spirit.

Understand the Truth

Living by the flesh is evidenced by falsehood, sinful anger and rage, stealing, foul language, bitterness, brawling, slander, malice, sexual immorality, obscenity, foolish talk, coarse joking, impurity and greed. Bad stuff. Someone living by the Spirit is speaking truth, letting go of anger, working and giving to others, using words that build up and benefit others. Living by the Spirit also produces kindness, compassion, forgiving others, loving others, thanksgiving, goodness, righteousness, truthfulness, and a desire to please the Lord. Anyone would want to know someone like this.

Reflect and Respond

THE CONFLICT BETWEEN THE SPIRIT AND THE FLESH

Read the Truth

Put to death, therefore, whatever belongs to your earthly nature: sexual immorality, impurity, lust, evil desires and greed, which is idolatry. Because of these, the wrath of God is coming. You used to walk in these ways, in the life you once lived. But now you must also rid yourselves of all such things as these: anger, rage, malice, slander, and filthy language from your lips. Do not lie to each other, since you have taken off your old self with its practices and have put on the new self, which is being renewed in knowledge in the image of its Creator. Here there is no Gentile or Jew, circumcised or uncircumcised, barbarian, Scythian, slave or free, but Christ is all, and is in all. Therefore, as God's chosen people, holy and dearly loved, clothe yourselves with compassion, kindness, humility, gentleness and patience. Bear with each other and forgive one another if any of you has a grievance against someone. Forgive as the Lord forgave you. And over all these virtues put on love, which binds them all together in perfect unity. (Colossians 3:5-14)

Confirm the Truth

From Colossians 3:5-14, what is the evidence of living by the flesh?

From Colossians 3:5-14, what is the evidence of living by the Spirit?

Understand the Truth

The evidence of living by the flesh once again is pretty obvious. Paul lists sexual immorality, impurity, lust, evil desires, greed, and idolatry plus anger, rage, malice, slander, filthy language, and lying. Often, we blame people or circumstances for our anger. People and circumstances do not cause our anger, impatience, bitterness, etc. Our reactions to people and circumstances reveal where we are living—by the Spirit or by the flesh.

The evidence of living by the Spirit is morality, compassion, kindness, humility, gentleness, patience, bearing with each other, forgiving each other, and loving each other. Although we no longer measure our way of living by the Law of Moses (including the Ten Commandments) which was given to Israel, the New Testament writers certainly gave us plenty of description of what sin looks like in a Christian's life! Living by the flesh is pretty ugly, isn't it? Would you say there is a stark contrast between the two lifestyles? The Christian life is not hard; it is impossible apart from Christ Himself.

Reflect and Respond

We all have areas of our own lives in which we are still living by the flesh. Don't feel alone. Which ones jumped out at you when you listed them? Jesus wants you to trust Him to live by the Spirit in those areas.

THE CONFLICT BETWEEN THE SPIRIT AND THE FLESH

Read the Truth

So I say, walk by the Spirit, and you will not gratify the desires of the flesh. (Galatians 5:16)

Rather, clothe yourselves with the Lord Jesus Christ, and do not think about how to gratify the desires of the flesh. (Romans 13:14)

Confirm the Truth

How do we overcome the flesh (Galatians 5:16)?

How do we overcome the flesh (Romans 13:14)?

Understand the Truth

You can make the choice to not gratify the desires of the flesh but to walk by the Spirit, in dependence on the Spirit to help you follow through with this choice. Paul writes in Romans 13 not to even think about how to gratify the desires of the flesh. Don't even go there!

Sin is ugly. Very ugly! Though we are a new creation in Christ, we still retain our old bodies in which sin dwells (the flesh or sinful nature). We are encouraged to live by the Spirit, yet we are warned that we can choose to live by the flesh which is at war within us, at war against the Spirit. Are we left helpless like a pawn in the midst of the conflict? No, we have God's empowering presence in us. He is able to help us win the battle over sin. But we have a responsibility as well.

Paul writes in Galatians 5:16, *"So I say, live by the Spirit, and you will not gratify the desire of the sinful nature."* Notice what this verse does **not** say. It does not say, "If you clean up the flesh, you will become spiritual" (the logic of legalism). It does not say, "The desires of the flesh will go away" (the logic of triumphalism). As long as we live in these unredeemed bodies, sin remains a source of temptation in us. But that should drive us to dependence on Christ, which is the best thing for us.

Reflect and Respond

SET FREE FROM THE POWER OF SIN

Read the Truth

In the same way, count yourselves dead to sin but alive to God in Christ Jesus. Therefore do not let sin reign in your mortal body so that you obey its evil desires. Do not offer any part of yourself to sin as an instrument of wickedness, but rather offer yourselves to God as those who have been brought from death to life; and offer every part of yourself to Him as an instrument of righteousness. For sin shall no longer be your master, because you are not under the law, but under grace. (Romans 6:11-14)

I am using an example from everyday life because of your human limitations. Just as you used to offer yourselves as slaves to impurity and to ever-increasing wickedness, so now offer yourselves as slaves to righteousness leading to holiness. When you were slaves to sin, you were free from the control of righteousness. What benefit did you reap at that time from the things you are now ashamed of? Those things result in death! But now that you have been set free from sin and have become slaves of God, the benefit you reap leads to holiness, and the result is eternal life. For the wages of sin is death, but the gift of God is eternal life in Christ Jesus our Lord. (Romans 6:19-23)

For the grace of God has appeared that offers salvation to all people. It teaches us to say "No" to ungodliness and worldly passions, and to live self-controlled, upright and godly lives in this present age... (Titus 2:11-12)

Confirm the Truth

What choices are identified for us in Romans 6:11-14?

What are the consequences of being slaves to sin (Romans 6:19-23)?

What benefits do we reap from being slaves of God (Romans 6:19-23)?

Paul tells believers we are no longer under law (which only shows us what we do wrong), but we are now under grace, which enables us to do what is right. According to Titus 2:11-12, what does grace do for us?

Understand the Truth

In Romans 6, Paul personifies sin as a slave master—a power that enslaves us. Roman Christians understood this concept well as 1 out of every 2 people in the Roman Empire was a literal slave. We may not have a slave society any longer. But what we may not realize is that every human being has a master and is a servant to something—either God and his righteousness or sin and its wickedness—no neutral ground. You might think you are your own master, but you're not. Self is really following the voice of master sin within.

All of our lives before Christ, the old slave master sin called the shots. When we believe in Jesus, **a greater power moves in**—the Holy Spirit. He **sets us free from the power** of that old slave master to become what God intended us to be. But we are not set free to be our own masters. That's not what it means to be set free. Our options are still: 1) sin or 2) God. We have a new master, the one who set us free—Jesus Christ.

Jesus is our master, but the old slave master still calls my name and calls your name. That old slave master yells pretty loudly sometimes. And we listen! Yet, we don't have to listen or carry out its orders. We are freed from sin's power over us because a greater power has moved in—God's Spirit—one who woos us to do right. How we yield to God's Spirit working in our lives is our choice.

The advice God has for you through Paul is to consider yourself dead to sin but alive to God. Do not let sin reign or rule in your mortal body to obey it. Do not offer parts of your body to sin as instruments of wickedness. Instead, you have the ability to offer every part of your body to God as instruments of righteousness. Recognize that sin is no longer your master as it once was. Realize that you got nothing good out of wickedness, and see that you get great benefits from righteous living.

Reflect and Respond

SET FREE FROM THE POWER OF SIN

Read the Truth

No temptation has overtaken you except what is common to mankind. And God is faithful; He will not let you be tempted beyond what you can bear. But when you are tempted, He will also provide a way out so that you can endure it. (1 Corinthians 10:13)

Confirm the Truth

What does God promise in 1 Corinthians 10:13 regarding temptation?

Based on what you have learned already, through whom does God give us the way of escape—through ourselves or through the Spirit's empowering presence within us?

Understand the Truth

All temptations that you experience are common to all humanity. The promise is that God will not let you be tempted beyond what you can bear. He will provide a way out so you can stand up under it. That way out is through the Spirit's empowering presence in you. The Spirit enables you to say "no" to temptation.

Whether or not we are presently tempted in a given area, we are capable of committing any sin mentioned in the Bible, given the right set of circumstances, time and opportunity. The progression is this:

- A received thought produces familiarity.
- Continued pondering produces a loss of repugnance and, eventually, curiosity.
- Desires, sometimes a total surprise, are generated to experiment. The most damaging or dangerous are the ones that blindside you with a desire you didn't even know you were capable of! So protect yourself at all times through prayer, "Lord, protect me from myself!"
- Having tried the activity, the flesh (like a goat) can learn to like, and even grow dependent, on any sensual stimulus.

Conclusion: We never outgrow our need to depend 100% upon Jesus Christ. Recognizing this should lead us to have compassion on one another (Galatians 6:1) and to not take risks with sinful behavior!

Every believer has a choice. If something is causing you to stumble in your following of Jesus, you have the freedom to choose not to continue interacting with that thing. If it's political arguments, you can choose to stop engaging in political conversations. If it's pornography, you can turn off your

197

computer. If it's money woes, you can choose the security of faith over the security of coin. The bottom line is, we have the power to remove obstacles and run a smooth race (Hebrews 12:1). ... God will always provide grace for sin and choice for temptation. There is always a way out of temptation (see 1 Corinthians 10:13). You just have to choose it. If you want to be mentally and emotionally free, that is. (John Newton, *Growing Young* blog, "Lessons Learned")

A habit is easier to maintain than it is to start. Faith can be a habit—a good habit. Make wise decisions to protect yourself. Protect your mind. Desires of the flesh do not go away. They are, however, like a fire in that they can burn hot or burn down, depending on whether you are feeding them. Don't play with fire. Make policy decisions to keep your distance from what tempts you.

Martin Luther, the priest who initiated the Protestant Reformation in the 1500s, described it this way,

> I cannot keep the birds from flying around my head; but by the grace of God I can keep them from building nests in my hair. (Martin Luther)

Reflect and Respond

What decisions are you making or should you make to protect yourself from what tempts you?

DAY 123

GRACE-MOTIVATED OBEDIENCE

Dealing with failure: "What should I do when I sin?"

Read the Truth

Therefore, there is now no condemnation for those who are in Christ Jesus... (Romans 8:1)

All this is from God, who reconciled us to Himself through Christ and gave us the ministry of reconciliation: that God was reconciling the world to Himself in Christ, not counting people's sins against them. And He has committed to us the message of reconciliation...God made Him who had no sin to be sin for us, so that in Him we might become the righteousness of God. (2 Corinthians 5:18-19, 21)

In Him we have redemption through His blood, the forgiveness of sins, in accordance with the riches of God's grace... (Ephesians 1:7)

When you were dead in your sins and in the uncircumcision of your flesh, God made you alive with Christ. He forgave us all our sins, having canceled the charge of our legal indebtedness, which stood against us and condemned us; He has taken it away, nailing it to the cross. (Colossians 2:13-14)

Confirm the Truth

What is true about all those in Christ (Romans 8:1)?

What is true about our sins in 2 Corinthians 5:18-19, 21?

What is true about our sins in Ephesians 1:7?

What is true about our sins in Colossians 2:13-14?

199

Understand the Truth

How long do you think you can go without sinning, without doing something that is a work of the flesh? Six days? Six hours? Can most of us go 6 minutes without having impure thoughts or selfish behavior—even unintentional and unrecognized? God understands this about us. Because we still retain our old bodies in which sin dwells, **we will sin**—unintentionally as well as deliberately.

All sin is disobeying God, whether unintentional or deliberate. All sin is covered by Christ's work on the cross—whether unintentional or deliberate. All sin is forgiven before it is ever committed (you **have** forgiveness)—whether unintentional or deliberate. Your sins were nailed to the cross. There is now no condemnation for anyone in Christ Jesus because God is no longer counting your sins against you and has placed all of them on Jesus Christ. You receive His righteousness instead, making you perfectly acceptable to God.

Reflect and Respond

GRACE-MOTIVATED OBEDIENCE

Read the Truth

For we do not have a high priest who is unable to empathize with our weaknesses, but we have one who has been tempted in every way, just as we are—yet He did not sin. Let us then approach God's throne of grace with confidence, so that we may receive mercy and find grace to help us in our time of need. (Hebrews 4:15-16)

In the same way, the Spirit helps us in our weakness. We do not know what we ought to pray for, but the Spirit Himself intercedes for us through wordless groans. (Romans 8:26)

Confirm the Truth

What assurance do you receive in Hebrews 4:15-16 that God does not cut Himself off from you when you are in a time of need?

What assurance do you receive in Romans 8:26 that God does not cut Himself off from you when you are weak?

Understand the Truth

God's throne is open to every believer for grace and help in our time of need, which certainly includes while we are weak from sin's influence. The Holy Spirit is interceding for us in our weakness, which includes sin. The Spirit does not stop speaking to us or working on us just because we do not want to listen. The fruit of thinking that every time you sin you have broken your fellowship with God is tremendous guilt and insecurity. This is living by law rather than by grace. Because of what Christ did on the cross, you are set free from fear of God because of sin, you can bask in His amazing love, and you can gratefully serve Him.

Remembering who you are in Christ can help you recognize and avoid two errors in thinking regarding your sin that stem from the logic of legalism: 1) when you sin (regardless of what it is), God cuts off fellowship from you until you repent, and 2) a believer's sins build up until she confesses them and asks for forgiveness.

The first error in thinking ignores the fact that Christ is both *in us* and considers us *in Him*. Nothing in our radical identity even opens the possibility of being alienated from God! If you are deliberately living by the flesh rather than by the Spirit in your life, you may choose to cut yourself off from praying to your God, reading the Bible, and community with other Christians. But that is not God cutting Himself out of you. You belong to God forever.

The second error in thinking also is evidence of living by law. What is the fruit of teaching that our sins build up until we confess them to receive forgiveness? It is guilt, worry, and time spent trying to stay "confessed up."

201

We envision God erasing the "not guilty" verdict on us and considering us "guilty" until we confess and are declared not guilty again. What's the difference between that and the Old Testament system of sacrifices where sins would build up between trips to the altar? Nothing!

Realistically, we probably won't recognize even half of our sins in a lifetime of being a believer. It's not biblical to think that we can do so, and teach that we have to do so, in order to maintain forgiveness or fellowship with God. By the way, just saying to God every day, "I confess all the sins I've done lately" is not what He's after. He's after a transformed life. That's why He went through all this trouble to give us a new identity.

Knowing you already have forgiveness leads to confidence, peace, joy and freedom. **Remember and rest** in your acceptance in Christ because of His finished work on the cross. And seek to live by the Spirit every day, which pleases the God who gave you this gift.

Reflect and Respond

GRACE-MOTIVATED OBEDIENCE

Read the Truth

Search me, God, and know my heart; test me and know my anxious thoughts. See if there is any offensive way in me, and lead me in the way everlasting. (Psalm 139:23-24)

Confirm the Truth

Based upon Psalm 139:23-24, what should be our heart attitude toward God regarding sin in our lives?

Understand the Truth

David's openness to God invited Him to examine him completely and regularly. David wanted to know where his life did not please God and wanted God to show him what to change. This should be our heart attitude toward God regarding any sin in our lives.

God wanted to remove the sin barrier between Him and you permanently. He's interested in you spending your time and effort producing fruit for Him to reflect His glory as He designed humanity to live. The righteous live by faith—in a God—whose grace defies our attempt—to still "measure up" (live by law) in some way. You should be thanking Him daily for His forgiveness and His love and acceptance of you in Christ and the opportunity you have to live a radically different kind of life. What an outstanding privilege this new identity is!

Sin can no longer enslave you unwillingly because there's a **competing and greater power—God Himself— in us**. Transforming power in your heart has set you free to produce His fruit. Living by the Spirit reveals to you through the Word and through prayer what is sin in your life and helps your repentant heart follow through with your desire for change.

Reflect and Respond

GRACE-MOTIVATED OBEDIENCE

The biblical way for dealing with recognized sin in our lives

Understand the Truth

STEP ONE: VIEW YOURSELF RIGHTLY.

Your identity is not "_____" (coveter, greedy, gossiper, whatever it is). You are in Christ, a child of God, who sometimes "_____" (covets, is greedy, gossips).

STEP TWO: RECOGNIZE (CONFESS) THE TRUTH REGARDING YOUR SIN.

To confess biblically means to agree with God about what you and He both know to be true. Confession is not a formula, a process, or dependent on a mediator. Regarding sin in your life, it is not saying, "I'm sorry." It is saying, "I agree with you, God. I blew it!" See your sin as ugly and awful!

> Use coveting for example: while reading Philippians 4:12 ("I have learned the secret of being content in any and every situation..."), the Spirit convicts you that you have been coveting rather than being content. You agree with God that your coveting is actually not being content with His provision. Coveting doesn't fit someone who knows God. That is confession.

STEP THREE: CONFESSION IS INCOMPLETE WITHOUT REPENTANCE.

Repentance means to change your mind about that sin, to mourn its ugliness, resulting in changing your actions. Paul calls that godly sorrow in 2 Corinthians 7:9-11 ("Godly sorrow brings repentance that leads to salvation and leaves no regret..."). Godly sorrow is saying, "I recognize what I am doing is wrong. This fills me with sorrow because it hurts You, God. Please help me to live differently." He will certainly do that! That's how our lives get transformed.

> Use coveting for example: You want to not covet any longer, and you want to be content and grateful for what God has already provided. So you pray, "Lord Jesus, please have your Spirit nudge me when I want to covet. Replace my coveting with contentment and gratitude. By faith, Lord, I want you to do that in my life." That is repentance.

Repentance isn't repentance **until you change something**. You can confess "until the cows come home" (daily, habitually) and never change anything. Jesus called for people to "repent" not "confess."

STEP FOUR: REPENTANCE LEADS TO DEPENDENCE.

Depend on the living Christ inside you for that change to take place. Our Lord Jesus Christ is not interested in our compliance (outward conformity) as much as He desires our obedience from the heart.

> Use coveting for example: Memorize Philippians 4:12-13 and any other scriptures that deal with being thankful for God's provision. Be sensitive to the Spirit's nudging when you are tempted to covet. Choose to be thankful instead.

Reflect and Respond

Is there any ugliness in your life that you mourn? Follow the steps above to live in freedom from that ugliness. What will you trust the living Christ inside you to do for you in that area?

GRACE-MOTIVATED OBEDIENCE

Read the Truth

So Christ Himself gave the apostles, the prophets, the evangelists, the pastors and teachers, to equip His people for works of service, so that the body of Christ may be built up until we all reach unity in the faith and in the knowledge of the Son of God and become mature, attaining to the whole measure of the fullness of Christ. (Ephesians 4:11-13)

11 We have much to say about this, but it is hard to make it clear to you because you no longer try to understand. 12 In fact, though by this time you ought to be teachers, you need someone to teach you the elementary truths of God's word all over again. You need milk, not solid food! 13 Anyone who lives on milk, being still an infant, is not acquainted with the teaching about righteousness. (Hebrews 5:11-13)

14 But solid food is for the mature, who by constant use have trained themselves to distinguish good from evil. 1 Therefore let us move beyond the elementary teachings about Christ and be taken forward to maturity... (Hebrews 5:14-6:1a)

Confirm the Truth

Christ gives the Church pastors and teachers for what purpose (Ephesians 4:11-13)?

What does the writer of Hebrews say about someone who refuses to grow spiritually (Hebrews 5:11-13)?

What does the writer of Hebrews say about someone who is growing spiritually (Hebrews 5:14-6:1a)?

Understand the Truth

What is a realistic view of spiritual growth? The Lord Jesus said He came to give us abundant life (John10:10), and the whole New Testament speaks in lavish terms about the quality of life God wants His children to experience. We are exhorted to press on to maturity in Christ. But how is spiritual growth recognized?

Spiritual growth is *not* growing 'more and more of me' so I need 'less and less of Christ.' It is growing in knowledge and experience as we walk with Him, discovering more and more our need to depend totally on Him.

205

Growth is gradual. There is a common misconception that one's life is either 100% "carnal'" (living by the flesh) or 100% "spiritual" (living by the Spirit) at any given time. In fact, probably every believer is trusting Christ with some aspects of his life *at the same time and right alongside other areas of his life where he is living in self-sufficiency.* Growth, therefore, involves Christ progressively teaching us to trust Him in new unexplored areas of our lives, and deepening our sense of dependency in areas where we have previously grown a little.

You don't become more aware of your own "holiness" as you grow. On the contrary, the voices of the saints through history consistently agree that as you grow you become more aware of *how far short you fall from true holiness.* You become *more* aware of your sinfulness as you grow, *not less.*

Understanding these things underscores our need to understand the grace of God in Jesus Christ, and our identity in him. Only because of the Lord's grace can we grow in self-knowledge and handle the ongoing struggle against the world, the flesh, and the devil. We would sooner or later throw in the towel without our assurance of His continued acceptance, teaching, and kindness. (Tim Stevenson, *T.E.A.M. Training,* Session 17)

Spiritual growth involves God growing us, stretching us, and reconstructing us because He loves us and lives in us and desires that we be transformed into the likeness of His Son. It's for our good and His glory! Praise Jesus for working out your salvation in such a personal way.

Reflect and Respond

Looking at your life, reflect on your growth over time. In what areas have you learned to trust Christ more?

In what areas have you recently become more aware of your sinfulness?

part 10

GRACE CALLS FOR YOU TO FOLLOW

Whoever serves me must follow me; and where I am, my servant also will be. My Father will honor the one who serves me. (JOHN 12:26)

DAY 128

FOLLOWING JESUS AS HIS DISCIPLE

Read the Truth

As Jesus was getting into the boat, the man who had been demon-possessed begged to go with Him. (Mark 5:18)

"What do you want me to do for you?" Jesus asked him. The blind man said, "Rabbi, I want to see." "Go," said Jesus, "your faith has healed you." Immediately he received his sight and followed Jesus along the road. (Mark 10:51-52)

*Jesus Christ said, "I have come that they may have life, and have it to the full." (John 10:10) He said on another occasion, "Come to me, all you who are weary and burdened, and I will give you rest. Take my yoke upon you and learn from me, for I am gentle and humble in heart, and **you will find rest for your souls**. For my yoke is easy and my burden is light." (Matthew 11:28-30)*

Confirm the Truth

In Mark 5:18, what does the healed man want to do?

In Mark 10:52, what does the healed man do?

In Matthew 11:28-30, what does Jesus promise to those who follow Him as His disciple?

Understand the Truth

In Matthew, Jesus said those who followed Him would receive rest from their weariness and heavy burdens.

"Yoke" refers to the harness that connected a pair of animals, usually oxen, to a plow. The yoke linked them together so they could work efficiently. Often a young animal was paired with an older one, allowing the younger one to learn "on the job" from the experienced animal. In New Testament times, the phrase "take the yoke of" was used by the Jewish rabbis to mean, "become the pupil of a certain teacher," in this case the disciple of Jesus. (*Illustrated Dictionary of the Bible,* p. 1066)

As we have seen so far in this study, the *rest* Jesus offers is from the work of the Law (plus all the additional burdens Israel's spiritual leaders had loaded onto the people) in order to maintain a right standing with God. This invitation recalls Jeremiah 31:25 where the Lord offered His people rest in the New Covenant ("I will refresh the weary and satisfy the faint"). Jesus, the revealer of God, invites those who long to know God and be refreshed in life to come to Him. Jesus' burden is light compared to the loads other religious leaders impose on their followers.

Both men who had been healed of their diseases and given new life wanted to follow Jesus. To follow means to follow where He is going and to learn from Him. Jesus wants everyone who trusts in Him as Savior and Lord to become one of His "disciples." A disciple is an active follower or learner. A disciple studies the teachings of another person whom they respect and applies those teachings to her life. Anyone who recognizes how much they have been forgiven should want to follow Jesus today.

That includes you. Jesus Christ calls you to **intentionally** follow Him as His disciple. This means committing to learning from Him and becoming like Him as you obediently apply what He teaches you through His book, the Bible, and what He allows into your life. Have you made the decision to follow Him?

Reflect and Respond

FOLLOWING JESUS AS HIS DISCIPLE

Read the Truth

Therefore everyone who hears these words of mine and puts them into practice is like a wise man who built his house on the rock. The rain came down, the streams rose, and the winds blew and beat against that house; yet it did not fall, because it had its foundation on the rock. But everyone who hears these words of mine and does not put them into practice is like a foolish man who built his house on sand. The rain came down, the streams rose, and the winds blew and beat against that house, and it fell with a great crash. (Matthew 7:24-27)

To the Jews who had believed Him, Jesus said, "If you hold to my teaching, you are really my disciples. Then you will know the truth, and the truth will set you free." (John 8:31-32)

So Christ Himself gave the apostles, the prophets, the evangelists, the pastors and teachers, to equip His people for works of service, so that the body of Christ may be built up until we all reach unity in the faith and in the knowledge of the Son of God and become mature, attaining to the whole measure of the fullness of Christ. Then we will no longer be infants, tossed back and forth by the waves, and blown here and there by every wind of teaching and by the cunning and craftiness of people in their deceitful scheming. (Ephesians 4:11-14)

Confirm the Truth

What are the benefits of putting God's truth into practice (building on the rock) according to Matthew 7:24-27?

What are the benefits of learning from Jesus and applying what you learn (John 8:31-32)?

Based on Ephesians 4:11-14, what are the benefits of learning God's truth and putting it into practice?

Understand the Truth

Learning from Jesus involves being a student of His Word (our Bible) and choosing to put God's truth into practice as a lifestyle. There are wonderful benefits of doing so. You will have a solid foundation for your life that will enable you to withstand the storms of life. You will know truth and experience

freedom from the bondage to error and all the chaos error can produce in your life. You will no longer be tossed back and forth by every wind of teaching and the cunning ways of deceitful men or women. Your life will be characterized by peace, stability and strength regardless of circumstances. This stems from your choice to become Jesus' disciple.

Reflect and Respond

Confidence in God's Word

Read the Truth

Then Jesus was led by the Spirit into the wilderness to be tempted by the devil. After fasting forty days and forty nights, He was hungry. The tempter came to Him and said, "If you are the Son of God, tell these stones to become bread." Jesus answered, "It is written: 'Man shall not live on bread alone, but on every word that comes from the mouth of God.'" Then the devil took Him to the holy city and had Him stand on the highest point of the temple. "If you are the Son of God," he said, "throw yourself down. For it is written: 'He will command His angels concerning you, and they will lift you up in their hands, so that you will not strike your foot against a stone.'" Jesus answered him, "It is also written: 'Do not put the Lord your God to the test.'" Again, the devil took Him to a very high mountain and showed Him all the kingdoms of the world and their splendor. "All this I will give you," he said, "if you will bow down and worship me." Jesus said to him, "Away from me, Satan! For it is written: 'Worship the Lord your God, and serve Him only.'" Then the devil left Him, and angels came and attended Him. (Matthew 4:1-11)

He went to Nazareth, where He had been brought up, and on the Sabbath day He went into the synagogue, as was His custom. He stood up to read, and the scroll of the prophet Isaiah was handed to Him. Unrolling it, He found the place where it is written: "The Spirit of the Lord is on me, because He has anointed me to proclaim good news to the poor. He has sent me to proclaim freedom for the prisoners and recovery of sight for the blind, to set the oppressed free, to proclaim the year of the Lord's favor." Then He rolled up the scroll, gave it back to the attendant and sat down. The eyes of everyone in the synagogue were fastened on Him. He began by saying to them, "Today this scripture is fulfilled in your hearing." (Luke 4:16-21)

For you have been born again, not of perishable seed, but of imperishable, through the living and enduring word of God. For, "All people are like grass, and all their glory is like the flowers of the field; the grass withers and the flowers fall, but the word of the Lord endures forever." And this is the word that was preached to you. (1 Peter 1:23-25)

Confirm the Truth

How did Jesus use the Old Testament scriptures ("it is written") in Matthew 4:1-11?

How did Jesus use the Old Testament scriptures in Luke 4:16-21?

What is revealed about the Word of God in 1 Peter 1:23-25?

Understand the Truth

Jesus knew the Old Testament Scriptures (the revealed Word of God) well and used them in His life and ministry. The New Testament was not yet written so when He refers to the Scriptures, He is referring to what we know as the Old Testament.

Jesus used Bible verses that He had memorized to defeat Satan's temptations in the desert. He used a specific passage of the book of Isaiah when He preached in His hometown of Nazareth. The verses He chose to read referenced the promises about the Messiah's coming. Jesus declared that He was the fulfillment of those biblical promises.

Peter described the Word of God embodied in Jesus Christ and the Gospel message as living and enduring; it stands forever.

The Bible is an amazing book. It was written over a 1,500-year period by about 40 different authors living in several different countries. It was written in three different languages—Hebrew, Aramaic and Greek. Yet the Bible is consistent in its central theme and key figure—it focuses upon Jesus Christ. Such a feat would be impossible without one supreme Author—the Holy Spirit of God. We can have complete confidence in it!

Reflect and Respond

213

CONFIDENCE IN GOD'S WORD

Read the Truth

All Scripture is God-breathed and is useful for teaching, rebuking, correcting and training in righteousness... (2 Timothy 3:16)

Above all, you must understand that no prophecy of Scripture came about by the prophet's own interpretation of things. For prophecy never had its origin in the human will, but prophets, though human, spoke from God as they were carried along by the Holy Spirit. (2 Peter 1:20-21)

Confirm the Truth

In 2 Timothy 3:16, what did Paul declare about the Scriptures?

In 2 Peter 1:20-21, what did Peter declare about the words of the prophets in the Scriptures?

Understand the Truth

Paul said the Scriptures were God-breathed. This is what that means: what was written by people was breathed out by God. He spoke through men and women as His spokesmen. Peter said that the writers spoke from God as they were carried along by the Holy Spirit. God-driven. God-breathed.

> God-breathed doesn't mean that the writers of the Scriptures were sleep-walking. What it means is that God used their personalities, their abilities, their understanding, their talents and the real-life situations they were in to bring forth the Scripture that He wanted. Most of the New Testament letters were written to deal with circumstances. God is perfectly able to work through real-life circumstances in a real-life person like Paul, for example, to bring about the end result that He intends to use for the next however many centuries for us. (Tim Stevenson, *TEAM Training*, Session 3)

In 1 Peter 2:2, Peter encouraged all believers to "long for the pure milk of the Word." Milk is essential food for a baby to grow and develop properly. Likewise, the Scriptures (Old and New Testaments) are essential food for every believer to grow and develop into maturity.

Reflect and Respond

Is this how you view the Scriptures—as essential food for your life? Do you long for the Word every day? Ask God to give you an insatiable longing for His Word and to draw you to Himself through reading it.

214

CONVICTIONS BASED ON GOD'S WORD

Read the Truth

See to it that no one takes you captive through hollow and deceptive philosophy, which depends on human tradition and the elemental spiritual forces of this world rather than on Christ. (Colossians 2:8)

Do not conform to the pattern of this world, but be transformed by the renewing of your mind. Then you will be able to test and approve what God's will is—His good, pleasing and perfect will. (Romans 12:2)

We demolish arguments and every pretension that sets itself up against the knowledge of God, and we take captive every thought to make it obedient to Christ. (2 Corinthians 10:5)

Confirm the Truth

From Colossians 2:8, what can take someone captive apart from Christ?

In order to not be taken captive by such philosophies, what should you do according to Romans 12:2?

What advice is given in 2 Corinthians 10:5 to keep you on the right path?

Understand the Truth

Paul says that you need to be careful not to be taken captive by hollow and deceptive philosophies that are derived from human traditions or reasonings and the elementary principles of this world. Examples of these could include anything that puts human ideas above God's ideas, the pursuit of personal happiness regardless of who gets hurt in the process, anything that promises prosperity, reliance on any source of spirituality other than the God of the Bible, or declaring no need for God at all. All these ideas set themselves up against the knowledge of God.

So in order to not be taken captive by such deceptive teaching, you can make the choice to not conform any longer to the pattern of this world (what your culture wants you to do) but be transformed by the renewing of your mind (Romans 12:2). As we have seen on previous days, you renew your mind through knowing the Bible, which is God's truth (John 8:31-32), and through the Holy Spirit

215

implanting that truth in your mind so you can understand it (1 Corinthians 2:9-16). With a firm hold on God's truth, you can diffuse arguments against the knowledge of God that are influencing you, and you can take captive your thoughts, making them obedient to Christ.

God and the devil agree on one thing: Both want to capture your *mind,* because whoever captures your mind will direct the course of your life. Everyone maintains a number of *premises* for living, both consciously and unconsciously. Premises are assumptions that form the foundation and shape of your thinking. They are important because of a universal law of logic and behavior: "If your premise is off, your findings will be off." The actions you take will not likely succeed.

God wants your values, beliefs, and convictions to be formed by His Word. Biblical convictions can be compared to the policies of an organization. Like policies, convictions provide a measure of protection against danger by establishing safe boundaries. Convictions also eliminate needless decision-making by settling many issues in advance, thereby enabling greater consistency, efficiency, and productivity. Because biblical convictions are based on an objective standard of truth (the Word of God), they provide a reliable standard for daily decision-making, as opposed to living by fickle emotions.

Reflect and Respond

CONVICTIONS BASED ON GOD'S WORD

Read the Truth

But the Advocate, the Holy Spirit, whom the Father will send in my name, will teach you all things and will remind you of everything I have said to you. (John 14:26)

I have much more to say to you, more than you can now bear. But when He, the Spirit of truth, comes, He will guide you into all the truth. He will not speak on His own; He will speak only what He hears, and He will tell you what is yet to come. He will glorify me because it is from me that He will receive what He will make known to you. All that belongs to the Father is mine. That is why I said the Spirit will receive from me what He will make known to you. (John 16:12-15)

[God] Sanctify them by the truth; your word is truth. (John 17:17)

Confirm the Truth

According to John 14:26, what was the Holy Spirit's role in supervising the apostles' teaching and writing so that we may have confidence in the reliability of the New Testament?

What do Jesus' words about the Holy Spirit's work in John 16:12-15 add to our confidence in the reliability of the New Testament?

What is truth according to Jesus in John 17:17?

Understand the Truth

Jesus told His disciples that the Holy Spirit would remind the apostles of all that Jesus taught them. And the Spirit would speak to the apostles all that Jesus wants made known to them. Jesus would continue to reveal Himself and the truth He wants all His followers to know. The writings of the New Testament are the work of the Holy Spirit revealing Himself to the apostles and other disciples of Jesus.

There are 5,686 Greek manuscripts in existence today for the New Testament. If we were to compare the number of New Testament manuscripts to other ancient writings, we find that...there are thousands more New Testament Greek manuscripts than any other ancient writing. The internal consistency of the New Testament documents is about 99.5% textually pure. That is an amazing accuracy. In addition, there are over 19,000 copies in the Syriac, Latin, Coptic, and Aramaic languages. The total supporting New Testament manuscript base is over 24,000...The Christian has substantially superior criteria for affirming the New Testament documents than he does for any other ancient writing. It is good evidence on which to base the trust in the reliability of the New Testament. (Matt Slick, "Manuscript evidence for superior New Testament reliability," http://carm.org/manuscript-evidence)

The historical reliability of the Scriptures is an important issue, and they (the Scriptures) can be investigated to show that the biblical records are trustworthy. Biblical convictions are based upon what God has revealed about Himself. And we know that God's Word is true and reliable. From our study so far, we know that the Bible asserts that man can truly know God and know truth about Him. However, because man is finite, His knowledge of God can never be comprehensive.

*"The secret things belong to the LORD our God, but the things revealed **belong to us** and to our children forever, that we may follow all the words of this law." (Deuteronomy 29:29)*

There will be things that you cannot know ("the secret things") or concepts you may not understand right now. You must humbly accept that. But we CAN KNOW what has been revealed. God has revealed in His Word much truth about Him and His way of approaching life. Dwell on what you can know. Make your "home" there in your thoughts and guidance for living.

Reflect and Respond

We live in a world of controversy and diverse worldviews. Having an objective standard of truth can be both a shield and a weapon (Proverbs 30:5, 2 Corinthians 10:5).

Do you have confidence in the reliability of the Scriptures? If you have come across certain parts of scripture that you don't understand or can't know the answer, are you willing to humbly accept that?

TAKING EVERY THOUGHT CAPTIVE

Read the Truth

"We demolish arguments and every pretension that sets itself up against the knowledge of God, and we take captive every thought to make it obedient to Christ." (2 Corinthians 10:5)

Confirm the Truth

Considering Paul's advice in 2 Corinthians 10:5, what would it look like for you to take captive every thought and make it obedient to Christ?

What could be the benefits to you when you take every thought captive and make it obedient to Christ?

Understand the Truth

Living in intentional cooperation with the Spirit as He transforms you into the image of Christ involves the practice of "taking every thought captive" to Christ as exhorted by Paul. When you begin to understand this verse, you will discover a few things.

First, you need to pass everything that you believe, or that you think you should believe, through the grid of God's Word. Does it line up with the truth found in Scripture? God will help you recognize error in thinking.

Second, you do not have to entertain every thought that runs through your head on a daily basis. Because the Holy Spirit lives in you, you have the ability to discern God-pleasing thoughts from thoughts that grieve His heart. You can take those thoughts captive and replace them with truth from His Word.

Third, you do not have to be enslaved to emotions that are influenced by lies. The more you practice taking every thought captive to make it obedient to Christ, the freer you will be from the tyranny of your emotions. Your emotions will then be based on truth and will be beneficial to you.

Fourth, error in thinking will seriously affect your behavior and your relationships. The more you practice taking every thought captive to make it obedient to Christ, the more you will be transformed by the Spirit into a godly man or woman whose life is filled with love, joy, peace and the rest of the fruit God wants to produce in your life.

Over the next few days, we will examine commonly asked questions that reflect someone's values, beliefs, and convictions. We will take captive the error in thinking and replace it with truth that is obedient to Jesus Christ.

Reflect and Respond

Do you recognize certain areas of your thought life that you need to take captive and make obedient to Christ?

TAKE EVERY THOUGHT CAPTIVE

❦❧❦❧❦❧❦❧❦

Question #1: Where can I find meaning and purpose in life?

Error in thinking: Find it through people, places and things.

Read the Truth

I [Solomon] said to myself, "Come now, I will test you with pleasure to find out what is good." But that also proved to be meaningless. "Laughter," I said, "is madness. And what does pleasure accomplish?" I tried cheering myself with wine, and embracing folly—my mind still guiding me with wisdom. I wanted to see what was good for people to do under the heavens during the few days of their lives. I undertook great projects: I built houses for myself and planted vineyards. I made gardens and parks and planted all kinds of fruit trees in them. I made reservoirs to water groves of flourishing trees. I bought male and female slaves and had other slaves who were born in my house. I also owned more herds and flocks than anyone in Jerusalem before me. I amassed silver and gold for myself, and the treasure of kings and provinces. I acquired male and female singers, and a harem as well—the delights of a man's heart. I became greater by far than anyone in Jerusalem before me. In all this my wisdom stayed with me. I denied myself nothing my eyes desired; I refused my heart no pleasure. My heart took delight in all my labor, and this was the reward for all my toil. Yet when I surveyed all that my hands had done and what I had toiled to achieve everything was meaningless, a chasing after the wind; nothing was gained under the sun. (Ecclesiastes 2:1-11)

Jesus answered, "It is written: 'Man shall not live on bread alone, but on every word that comes from the mouth of God'" (Matthew 4:4)

Now this is eternal life: that they know you, the only true God, and Jesus Christ, whom you have sent. (John 17:3)

For we are God's handiwork, created in Christ Jesus to do good works, which God prepared in advance for us to do. (Ephesians 2:10)

Confirm the Truth

According to Ecclesiastes 2:1-11, what did Solomon learn about trying to find meaning and purpose in people, places, and things?

How do Jesus' words in Matthew 4:4 answer the question about how to find meaning and purpose in life?

What does Jesus say in John 17:3 that leads you to find meaning and purpose in life?

How do the words in Ephesians 2:10 help us find meaning and purpose in life?

Understand the Truth

A fundamental question about human life is asking, "Where do I find meaning and purpose in life?" The wrong answer is to find it through people, places, and things. Why is that wrong? Think about the effects of that thinking on your life. People let you down. Places change. Things get old and require maintenance time and money. Nothing will truly satisfy because something or someone will always look better than what you have. Solomon found that out.

Jesus said that we should "live" on God's Word and be satisfied in Him even more than the daily bread that sustains physical life. Meaning and purpose also comes through a relationship with God through Jesus Christ. And in this relationship, we realize the good works that God has created for us to do that will give our lives individual purpose.

Years ago, a very influential Christian leader declared this,

> ...you [God]have made us and drawn us to yourself, and our heart is unquiet until it rests in you. (Augustine of Hippo, *The Confessions*)

Where can anyone find meaning and purpose in life? The answer is through a relationship with Jesus Christ.

Reflect and Respond

Ask Jesus to help you understand this truth so you can be set free from error and provide answers to this question when asked by someone else.

221

TAKING EVERY THOUGHT CAPTIVE

Question #2: Are there objective standards of right and wrong?

Error in thinking: Right and wrong are relative; there are no absolutes.

Read the Truth

So I say, walk by the Spirit, and you will not gratify the desires of the flesh. For the flesh desires what is contrary to the Spirit, and the Spirit what is contrary to the flesh. They are in conflict with each other, so that you are not to do whatever you want. But if you are led by the Spirit, you are not under the law. The acts of the flesh are obvious: sexual immorality, impurity and debauchery; idolatry and witchcraft; hatred, discord, jealousy, fits of rage, selfish ambition, dissensions, factions and envy; drunkenness, orgies, and the like. I warn you, as I did before, that those who live like this will not inherit the kingdom of God. But the fruit of the Spirit is love, joy, peace, forbearance, kindness, goodness, faithfulness, gentleness and self-control. Against such things there is no law. (Galatians 5:16-23)

Confirm the Truth

How do you know there are objective standards of right and wrong in God's eyes based on Galatians 5:16-23?

Understand the Truth

Consider the effects of thinking that right and wrong are relative and that there are no absolutes. That thinking might lead to someone experimenting with evil in various areas of life because there are no standards to provide boundaries. It can also lead to emotional decision-making—whatever feels good, do it. Holding to relative right and wrong can also create a lot of confusion when people don't abide to the same standards of right and wrong. The logical conclusion to the thinking that there are no absolutes is denial of the rule of law. Yet, national laws usually say that some things are definitely wrong. Laws of society declare absolutes as being true. And the moment one declares there are no absolutes, he/she has just stated an absolute. So it's an illogical statement anyway.

The truth is that there is definite right and wrong in God's eyes. Galatians 5 is only one list of behaviors God declares to be right or wrong. Add to that list the behaviors found in Colossians 3 and Ephesians 4 and 5. The God who created everyone has the right to make the rules. Are there objective standards of right and wrong? The answer is, "Yes." The objective standard is from God and recorded in the Bible.

Reflect and Respond

Ask Jesus to help you understand this truth so you can be set free from error and provide answers to this question when asked by someone else.

TAKING EVERY THOUGHT CAPTIVE

Question #3: What is the source of human evil?

Error in thinking: It is the fault of others, or of circumstances.

Read the Truth

After He had left the crowd and entered the house, His disciples asked Him about this parable. "Are you so dull?" He asked. "Don't you see that nothing that enters a person from the outside can defile them? For it doesn't go into their heart but into their stomach, and then out of the body." (In saying this, Jesus declared all foods clean.) He went on: "What comes out of a person is what defiles them. For it is from within, out of a person's heart, that evil thoughts come—sexual immorality, theft, murder, adultery, greed, malice, deceit, lewdness, envy, slander, arrogance and folly. All these evils come from inside and defile a person." (Mark 7:17-23)

The heart is deceitful above all things and beyond cure. Who can understand it? (Jeremiah 17:9)

Confirm the Truth

According to Mark 7:17-23, what is the source of human evil?

According to Jeremiah 17:9, what is true about the human heart?

Understand the Truth

Anyone who thinks that people are born basically good and become evil because of the influence of others is naïve about the sin nature of humanity. It is very easy to start blaming everyone else for one's own mistakes, circumstances, and behavior. The Bible is totally clear that human evil originates in the heart of every person. All those wicked behaviors begin in the human heart before showing up externally. The heart is deceitful, deceiving even itself about how "good" it is in one's own eyes.

What is the heart? The *heart* in the Scripture is used sometimes for the *mind and understanding*, sometimes for the *will*, sometimes for the *affections*, sometimes for the *conscience*, sometimes for the *whole soul of man*.

Scripture clearly teaches us that the real issues of life are spiritual and are really matters of the heart, the inner man. Maybe it's for this reason the word "heart" is found so many times in the Bible...When used metaphorically (depending on the context) *heart* refers to either the mind, the emotions, the will, to the sinful nature, *inclusively* to the total inner man, or simply to the person as a whole and is often translated as such...The term heart, then, generally speaks of **the inner person** and the

223

spiritual life in all its various aspects. (J. Hampton Keathley, III, "Guarding Your Heart," accessed at www.bible.org)

So what is the source of human evil? It is the inner person of every human.

Reflect and Respond

Ask Jesus to help you understand this truth so you can be set free from error and provide answers to this question when asked by someone else.

TAKE EVERY THOUGHT CAPTIVE

Question #4: What if I choose to do wrong anyway?

Error in thinking: I can do what I want without consequences.

Read the Truth

Do not be deceived: God cannot be mocked. A man reaps what he sows. Whoever sows to please their flesh, from the flesh will reap destruction; whoever sows to please the Spirit, from the Spirit will reap eternal life. (Galatians 6:7-8)

Confirm the Truth

According to Galatians 6:7-8, what will happen if you choose to do wrong anyway?

Understand the Truth

For those who think they can do whatever they want without consequences, their lives will be characterized by pride, coldness, and lack of compassion. Their reasoning about whether someone gets hurt or not is, "It's not my problem. It is theirs." Other effects of this kind of wrong thinking are poor decision-making and a life of regret.

The Bible is clear. God will not be mocked by the arrogant who think they can outsmart God with their bad behavior. God cannot be mocked in that way. What if you choose to do wrong anyway? You will reap destructive consequences from your choices. It's a fact.

Reflect and Respond

Ask Jesus to help you understand this truth so you can be set free from error and provide answers to this question when asked by someone else.

TAKE EVERY THOUGHT CAPTIVE

Question #5: Where can I find success and security?

Error in thinking: Find security in money and position. Seek success at any price.

Read the Truth

So do not worry, saying, 'What shall we eat?' or 'What shall we drink?' or 'What shall we wear?' For the pagans run after all these things, and your heavenly Father knows that you need them. But seek first His kingdom and His righteousness, and all these things will be given to you as well. (Matthew 6:31-33)

But godliness with contentment is great gain. For we brought nothing into the world, and we can take nothing out of it. But if we have food and clothing, we will be content with that. Those who want to get rich fall into temptation and a trap and into many foolish and harmful desires that plunge people into ruin and destruction. For the love of money is a root of all kinds of evil. Some people, eager for money, have wandered from the faith and pierced themselves with many griefs. (1 Timothy 6:6-10)

Confirm the Truth

What instruction did Jesus give in Matthew 6:31-33 about where you can find success and security?

According to 1 Timothy 6:6-10, how can you find success and security?

What are the dangers of seeking security and success through money?

Understand the Truth

The error in thinking that you find security in money and position and should seek success at any price can lead to disastrous results. These results might include cheating to get to the top, accumulating things and prestige as priority in life, and serious tanking when those things bringing "success and security" are taken away.

We are to find our security in our relationship with God and being part of God's kingdom. Seeking His righteousness will provide security and success in living a purposeful life. Godliness is devotion to God expressed in a life that is pleasing to Him. Money does not create nor maintain godliness. Contentment is a greater source of happiness and joy than prosperity ever could be. Where can you find success and security? Seek the Kingdom of God and His righteousness provided through faith in Jesus Christ. That will provide godliness with contentment.

Reflect and Respond

Ask Jesus to help you understand this truth so you can be set free from error and provide answers to this question when asked by someone else.

Take Captive Every Thought

Question #6: How can I become a person of influence?

Error in thinking: Climb the ladder upward over people and circumstances.

Read the Truth

Jesus called them together and said, "You know that the rulers of the Gentiles lord it over them, and their high officials exercise authority over them. Not so with you. Instead, whoever wants to become great among you must be your servant, and whoever wants to be first must be your slave—just as the Son of Man did not come to be served, but to serve, and to give His life as a ransom for many." (Matthew 20:25-28)

"Now I commit you to God and to the word of His grace, which can build you up and give you an inheritance among all those who are sanctified. I have not coveted anyone's silver or gold or clothing. You yourselves know that these hands of mine have supplied my own needs and the needs of my companions. In everything I did, I showed you that by this kind of hard work we must help the weak, remembering the words the Lord Jesus Himself said: 'It is more blessed to give than to receive.'" (Acts 20:32-35)

Confirm the Truth

From Matthew 20:25-28, how do you become a person of influence?

From Acts 20:32-35, how do you become a person of influence?

Understand the Truth

For those who think they must climb the ladder upward over people and circumstances in order to have influence, how might this affect their lives? That kind of thinking would produce cold-heartedness, meanness, loss of genuine relationships, lack of respect and compassion for people, and even cruelty. Those characteristics are opposite of what Jesus wants you to have as a person of influence. Jesus declared that the one who wants to be a respected influencer must be a servant to others—a servant leader. Paul talked about working hard to not be a burden to others and to help the weak in order to become a person of influence. Jesus is the greatest influencer who ever lived. He gave His life for the sake of others.

How can you become a person of influence? Serve and love others well.

Reflect and Respond

Ask Jesus to help you understand this truth so you can be set free from error and provide answers to this question when asked by someone else.

GRACE CALLS FOR YOU TO FOLLOW

Understand the Truth

In our society, we have so many options to obtain "knowledge" about how to live life—the education system, internet, television, movies, and books galore. Add to that whatever goes "viral!" Facebook posts, Pinterest boards, and other social media outlets grab our attention. Everyone expresses her own opinion about the latest issue of life, and society says all opinions are equally valuable. Hopefully, by now you have realized that thinking not based on scriptural truth can lead to some disastrous results.

To grow spiritually, you must pursue your relationship with God through Jesus Christ. Remember, Christianity **is** Christ! You make the decision to not only be a believer but also Jesus' disciple—someone who follows Him, learns from Him, and leads others to do the same. Choosing to become Jesus' disciple means you choose to:

- Listen to His speaking voice through the Word. *Hebrews 4:12*
- Speak back to Him from the heart in prayer. *1 Thessalonians 5:17*
- Maximize input of God's Word into your mind. *2 Timothy 3:14-17*
- Put truth into practice through obedience by faith. *James 1:22-25*
- Pursue relationships with other believers and disciples in the body of Christ. *Acts 2:42-47*
- Exercise your faith through serving others in Christ's name. *Philippians 2*
- Share your faith with nonbelievers and be willing to disciple new believers. *2 Timothy 2:2*

Surrender is a process—seek Him, sit with Him, surrender to Him. Purposely creating the time and space in your life to sit with God allows Him to nurture who you are, not only instruct you in what to do.

> Jesus asked the rich young ruler to surrender his fortune in order to know true riches (Mark 10:21). He asked the young boy to surrender his meager lunch so that thousands could feast (John 6:5-13). He asked the disciples to surrender their plans, their dreams, their very lives, to follow Him (Matthew 4:18-22, Luke 5:1-22). And He asks us to surrender our rights, our reputation, our possessions, and our security. He wants our dreams and desires, our losses and our loves. Why? [It's] because He knows that what He offers is better by far than anything we are holding onto. He knows that surrendering everything we have and everything we are to Him yields joy, purpose and peace that we cannot possess any other way. He knows that when we put our pain, loss and regret into His loving hands we will finally begin to experience the healing and the hope we long for." (Woven, *The Truth about Redemption Next Step*, "Redeeming Hope: Your journey Toward Surrender")

Reflect and Respond

Are you willing to respond to the call of God's grace in your life to be more than just a believer but to become a true disciple of Jesus, learning from Him and preparing yourself to lead others as well? Looking at the list above, what can you choose to do this week to become more of Jesus' disciple?

part 11

BECOME A GRACE-SHARER

*May the God of hope fill you with all joy and
peace as you trust in Him, so that you may
overflow with hope by the power of the Holy
Spirit.*

(ROMANS 15:13)

BECOME A GRACE-SHARER

Read the Truth

I have been crucified with Christ and I no longer live, but Christ lives in me. The life I now live in the body, I live by faith in the Son of God, who loved me and gave Himself for me. (Galatians 2:20)

For Christ's love compels us, because we are convinced that one died for all, and therefore all died. And He died for all, that those who live should no longer live for themselves but for Him who died for them and was raised again. (2 Corinthians 5:14-15)

Confirm the Truth

How should we now live as believers (Galatians 2:20)?

How does Christ's love for us compel us to live (2 Corinthians 5:14-15)?

Understand the Truth

Jesus Christ gave His life for you by grace, so He could give His life to you by grace, so He could live His life through you by grace. Knowing Christ's love for you and the presence of His life in you should motivate you to "live for Him" and to serve Him through serving others. Both are responses to God's grace in your life. This would include letting HIs life in you overflow to others around you, particularly those who need to know Christ.

> "Often we embrace grace, and then live according to works. If we choose to celebrate His grace and ALL of its implications as part of our daily worship, we become people who experience incredible joy and freedom that we LONG to give away!" (Judy Brower, *The Disciplemaking Ministry Guide for Women in Leadership*, "Navigate the Disciplemaking Pathway: Establish," p. 30)

As you have seen through this daily devotional, Jesus Christ calls you to a new life through faith in Him, clothes you with Himself, commissions you with a purpose to live for Him, and empowers you to fulfill that purpose through His indwelling Holy Spirit.

Reflect and Respond

Become a Grace-Sharer

Read the Truth

When He saw the crowds, He had compassion on them, because they were harassed and helpless, like sheep without a shepherd. Then He said to His disciples, "The harvest is plentiful but the workers are few. Ask the Lord of the harvest, therefore, to send out workers into His harvest field." (Matthew 9:36-38)

Confirm the Truth

From Matthew 9:36-38, how does Jesus feel about the crowds and why?

What does Jesus declare to His disciples about the harvest?

For what are His disciples to pray?

Understand the Truth

Jesus looked upon the crowds of people with compassion. He not only felt their need but also wanted to do something about it. He turned to His disciples to stress how important it was for them to likewise have compassion on the people who were feeling hopeless and rootless. The disciples were being called to be workers in the harvest, bringing the hope of Christ to the hopeless.

The evidences of human distress are everywhere around us. Women and men are in bondage to guilt, fear, destructive behavior, and fatigue due to the burden of responsibilities. Add to that erroneous views of God that leave them feeling empty, confused, and without meaning and purpose. Failure in relationships leaves people with a sense of rejection, worthlessness and extreme loneliness. Jesus Christ's plan to meet that need for every person is…Himself.

Reflect and Respond

BECOME A GRACE-SHARER

><8->7->8-><->8-><<->8-><<->8><

Read the Truth

18 Then Jesus came to them and said, "All authority in heaven and on earth has been given to me. 19 Therefore go and make disciples of all nations, baptizing them in the name of the Father and of the Son and of the Holy Spirit, 20 and teaching them to obey everything I have commanded you. And surely I am with you always, to the very end of the age." (Matthew 28:18-20)

Confirm the Truth

According to Matthew 28:18, what authority has Jesus been given?

Because He has the authority to commission His followers, what specific work does Jesus commission His followers to do in Matthew 28:19-20?

What is His promise to them (Matthew 28:20)?

Understand the Truth

To His followers, Jesus communicated His plan for meeting the spiritual needs of every person through "the Great Commission" (Matthew 28:18-20). The Great Commission has one single focus: **"Make disciples."** Jesus Christ chooses to accomplish the Great Commission through *people*—ordinary men and women like you and I as we are "going" about life sharing Christ by word and action to those around us, baptizing new believers as a symbolic proclamation of their new life inside, and teaching them who Christ is, what He accomplished on the cross for them, and how they can live out their new identity in Him.

MEN AND WOMEN WERE HIS METHOD.... It all started with Jesus calling a few men to follow Him. This revealed immediately the direction His evangelistic strategy would take. *His concern was not with programs to reach the multitudes, but with men whom the multitudes would follow*...what is more revealing about these men is that at first they do not impress us as being key men...Yet Jesus saw in these simple men the potential of leadership in the Kingdom. They were indeed 'unlearned and ignorant' according to the world's standard, but they were *teachable*...What is perhaps most significant about them was their sincere yearning for God and the realities of His life...Such men, pliable in the hands of the Master, could be

234

molded into a new image—*Jesus can use anyone who wants to be used.* (Robert E. Coleman, *The Master Plan of Evangelism*)

Jesus Christ gave this work to His followers—the very ones who watched Him make disciples of them. They saw Him do it! The men and women who followed Jesus knew what He was commissioning them to do. They experienced that relationship with Him that changed their own lives. So they were willing to bring that experience to the lost, hurting, hopeless populace in their neighborhoods, cities, and destinations. They brought good news that was real, relevant, and life-giving.

As you have seen Him change your own life, you can do this, also.

Reflect and Respond

235

BECOME A GRACE-SHARER

Read the Truth

² You yourselves are our letter, written on our hearts, known and read by everyone. ³ You show that you are a letter from Christ, the result of our ministry, written not with ink but with the Spirit of the living God, not on tablets of stone but on tablets of human hearts. (2 Corinthians 3:2-3)

Confirm the Truth

What does Paul call those who have responded to the gospel through his teaching in Corinth?

As a living "letter," how is this letter described?

Who reads such a living "letter" (verse 2)?

Understand the Truth

Jesus chooses to have His followers tell His story—what He did for them and through them. In essence, you become a *living letter* of Christ (2 Corinthians 3:2-3). Your story illustrates the power of Christ in your life. Your story allows you to become a **grace-sharer** as our Lord extended His grace to you. You have a story to share. You become a grace-sharer to those who listen to your story.

> People love to hear stories. This is evidenced by all the money that is spent watching movies, attending the theatre, buying books and by all the time that is spent watching the television. Telling your faith story is just that: your personal story about your faith. It's an unobtrusive way to speak about the love of God in your life and the love He has for all people...Your life and story is the best tract to be written! (*The Disciplemaking Ministry Guide for Women in Leadership*, "How to Share Your Faith," p. 21)

Reflect and Respond

What has Jesus done in your life that you wouldn't mind sharing with someone who wants to know?

DAY 146

SHARE YOUR STORY

There are several ways to look at telling your faith story. You may recall a dramatic event or specific point in time when you began a personal relationship with Jesus. So you remember well what it was like to not know Him and the difference He made in your life.

Or you may have grown up in the church and feel like you always knew who God was and trusted in Jesus as your Savior as a child. Those who trusted in Jesus as children often feel they "have nothing to tell" because they don't have a dramatic story. Yet, in the case of childhood believers, there occurs a later, mature decision to follow Christ as His disciple where more obvious life changes occurred. If you are in this category, therefore, focus on that later turning point in telling your story—when you made the decision to follow Jesus as His disciple at some point in your teen years or adult life—a childlike faith that becomes an adult faith.

By the way, what you might consider "nothing to tell" except your faithfulness to Christ through the years is what every Christian parent wants for her child to tell. You have a story to share!

Reflect and Respond

YOUR LIFE BEFORE KNOWING JESUS OR CHOOSING TO FOLLOW HIM

Use the questions below to get started.

What 2-3 words would you use to describe how you felt or what your greatest needs were at the time (e.g. loneliness, feelings of insignificance, anger, rejection)?

To what source did you look for security, peace of mind, or happiness?

How did those areas or activities begin to disappoint you or leave you unsatisfied?

Briefly share a personal example from your life that illustrates those needs and attitudes you just identified.

237

SHARE YOUR STORY

Reflect and Respond

HOW YOU CAME TO KNOW CHRIST (POINT OF SALVATION) OR CHOSE TO FOLLOW HIM

Use the questions below to continue writing your story.

How and when did you first hear the gospel and/or were exposed to Christianity or decided to follow Jesus?

What brought you to the place of being willing to listen or of wanting to be more than just a believer?

Who influenced you to follow Jesus?

Describe how you felt, what truths you heard, what you thought about them, how you felt after you made the decision.

SHARE YOUR STORY

Reflect and Respond

YOUR LIFE SINCE KNOWING JESUS AND CHOOSING TO FOLLOW HIM
Use the questions below to continue writing your story.
What pre-Christ heart needs have been satisfied by a relationship with Him?

How long did it take before you noticed any changes?

What does it look like in your life to have a relationship with Christ now?

Where do you struggle still?

How have you learned to trust Jesus through those struggles?

Briefly share a personal example from your life that illustrates the wonderful difference that Jesus Christ has made in your life.

239

DAY 149

PRAY AND LOVE

Read the Truth

I have revealed you to those whom you gave me out of the world. They were yours; you gave them to me and they have obeyed your word. Now they know that everything you have given me comes from you. For I gave them the words you gave me and they accepted them. They knew with certainty that I came from you, and they believed that you sent me. I pray for them. I am not praying for the world, but for those you have given me, for they are yours. (John 17:6-9)

*As you sent me into the world, I have sent them into the world. For them I sanctify myself, that they too may be truly sanctified. My prayer is not for them alone. **I pray also for those who will believe in me through their message**, that all of them may be one, Father, just as you are in me and I am in you. May they also be in us so that the world may believe that you have sent me. (John 17:18-21)*

Confirm the Truth

What did Jesus say about His disciples in John 17:6-9?

For whom did Jesus pray in John 17:18-21?

Understand the Truth

The night before He died, Jesus prayed in the garden for His disciples. He was confident they had received the truth of God and had believed in Jesus as the Son of God. He also prayed for all those who would believe through the message of His disciples (John 17:20). That included those who heard their preaching in the first century AD as well as all those who have read their teaching written in the New Testament. True believers through the years have shared the gospel over the past 2000 years down to this day. You are one of those who have believed because men and women have shared the good news of Jesus Christ so that you could know Jesus and, therefore, know God well.

Pray and watch for God to give you opportunity to share your story of life with Him. Courage and ability to share come through obedience. If you offer your story to Jesus and your willingness to share what He has done in your life, He will give you the courage to do so. This is another evidence of the grace God has given to you through Jesus Christ. Just say, "Yes!" Live intentionally as a GRACE-SHARER to those whom God places in your path.

Reflect and Respond

GRACEFUL LIVING TODAY

Read the Truth

May the God of hope fill you with all joy and peace as you trust in Him, so that you may overflow with hope by the power of the Holy Spirit. (Romans 15:13)

Confirm the Truth

When God fills you with all joy and peace, what is the result?

Understand the Truth

From the time sin entered into the relationship of all humans with our Creator God, the one question that continually demands an answer is, "How can guilty sinful man be made right in the eyes of a holy God?"

Humanity's spiritual problem can be compared to death caused by a fatal disease: (1) Sin ("the disease" Romans 3:23—all sinned) and (2) Death ("result of the disease" Romans 6:23—wages of sin). Our twofold problem demanded a twofold solution:

- For our sin disease, we need forgiveness and righteousness. *Answer: Christ's **death** (the cross).* We can now be cured of the disease.
- For our state of death, we need regeneration (the restoration of **life**). *Answer: Christ's **resurrection**.* We can now be given life that is forever.

The ultimate grace gift came—Jesus Christ—providing an answer to both spiritual problems. This is the Good News, the Gospel.

Jesus Christ **laid down** His life **for** you...so that He could **give** His life **to** you...so that He could **live** His life **through** you. (Ian Thomas, *The Saving Life of Christ*)

Because of the cross, you can dwell on the FACT that

- God was fully **satisfied** by Jesus' finished work on the cross.
- The barrier of sin has been taken away and complete **reconciliation** between you and God is possible.
- You have been purchased by the blood of Christ out of slavery to sin and released into freedom as God's act of **redemption**.
- You are completely **forgiven** of your sins, and Jesus cleanses your conscience from guilt.
- You have been declared righteous (**justified**) and are now perfectly acceptable to a holy God based on your faith in His Son.
- God declares you holy because of your faith in Christ. You are **sanctified**—set apart by Him and for Him.

Because of the resurrection, you can dwell on the FACT that you are made alive by the indwelling Holy Spirit **(regeneration)** who unites you to Christ so that "Christ in you" is a fact of your new existence. You are born again as a new creation in Christ with a new identity in Him.

With the restoration of life begins a new adventure. It was totally **God's work** to make sinners acceptable again in His sight. Our proper response is to **trust** and **rest in His work**, and to continually offer Him thanks from grateful hearts along with our willing service.

Jesus Christ calls you to a new life, clothes you with Himself, commissions you for a purpose (to be His disciple and to make disciples), and empowers you to fulfill that purpose through His Holy Spirit living inside of you.

Reflect and Respond

May the God of hope fill you with all joy and peace as you trust in Him so that you may "overflow with hope" while living this adventure of "Graceful Living" with Jesus today, tomorrow, and every future day of your life.

SOURCES

1. Augustine of Hippo, *The Confessions*
2. A.W. Tozer, *The Knowledge of the Holy*
3. Bob George, *Classic Christianity*
4. Charles Price, *Alive in Christ*
5. C.S. Lewis, *Mere Christianity*
6. Dr. Timothy Warner, *Resolving Spiritual Conflicts and Cross-Cultural Ministry, Freedom in Christ Ministries*
7. Dr. Tom Constable, *Constable's Notes on John*
8. Gordon Fee, *God's Empowering Presence: The Holy Spirit in the Letters of Paul*
9. Herbert Lockyear, Sr. Editor, *Illustrated Dictionary of the Bible*
10. J.B. Phillips, *Introduction to Letters to Young Churches*
11. John Calvin, *Calvin: Institutes of the Christian Religion*
12. John Hunter, *The Fall of Man*
13. John Newton, *Growing Young* blog, "Lessons Learned"
14. John R. W. Stott, *Understanding the Bible*
15. Martin Luther, comments on Romans 12
16. Matt Slick, "Manuscript evidence for superior New Testament reliability," accessed at http://carm.org/manuscript-evidence
17. Michelle Wallace, *"Fruit of the Vine: The Greatness of God," Living Magazine*, October 2012
18. *NIV Study Bible 1984 Edition*, Zondervan
19. N.T. Wright, *Jesus and the Victory of God: Christian Origins and the Question of God, Volume 2*
20. Oswald Chambers, *My Utmost for His Highest*, "The Staggering Question"
21. Philip Schaff, *History of the Christian Church, Volume 1*
22. Robert E. Coleman, *The Master Plan of Evangelism*
23. Tim Stevenson, *T.E.A.M. Training*
24. *The Disciplemaking Ministry Guide for Women in Leadership*, RESOUNDNOW
25. Tom Constable, *Dr. Constable's Notes on Romans*
26. *Vines Complete Expository Dictionary of Old and New Testament Words*
27. Woven, *The Truth about Redemption Next Step, "Redeeming Hope: Your journey Toward Surrender"*

www.ingramcontent.com/pod-product-compliance
Lightning Source LLC
Chambersburg PA
CBHW080750120626
46557CB00005B/1212